HELPING THEM TO LEARN

CURRICULUM ENTITLEMENT FOR CHILDREN WITH EMOTIONAL AND BEHAVIOURAL DIFFICULTIES

Edited by
PAUL COOPER

NASEN

– 6 FEB 2006

A NASEN Publication

Published in 1995

ISBN 0 906730 68 6

Published by NASEN Enterprises Ltd.
NASEN Enterprises is a company limited by guarantee, registered in England and Wales. Company No. 2637438.

Further copies of this book and details of NASEN's many other publications may be obtained from the Publications Department at its registered office:
2 Lichfield Road, Stafford ST17 4JX (Tel: 01785 46872 Fax: 01785 41187)

Copy editing by Nicola von Schreiber
Typeset in Times and printed in the United Kingdom by Impress Printers (Stoke-on-Trent) Ltd.

HELPING THEM TO LEARN
CURRICULUM ENTITLEMENT FOR CHILDREN WITH EMOTIONAL AND BEHAVIOURAL DIFFICULTIES

Contents

Page

Acknowledgement

The preparation of this book was aided by a grant from the Oxford University Department of Educational Studies.

Biographical Notes

The Editor

PAUL COOPER is a lecturer in the University of Cambridge Institute of Education, where he has a particular interest in the education of children with emotional and behavioural difficulties. Prior to this he held academic posts at the Universities of Birmingham and Oxford. He initially qualified in Scotland as an English teacher and taught for nine years in mainstream schools in Scotland and in a mainstream school and special facilities for pupils with EBD in England. He has published widely on the subject of EBD and other educational issues. He has written *Effective Schools for Disaffected Students* (Routledge: London, 1993), and *Emotional and Behavioural Difficulties: Theory to Practice* (Routledge: London, 1994, with Graham Upton and Colin Smith). He is currently editor of the journal *Therapeutic Care and Education.*

The Contributors

TRICIA BEAVIS is in charge of the Special Unit for children with EBD attached to Oughtonhead Junior School in Hitchen, Hertfordshire. Prior to working with children with EBD she taught in mainstream schools in New Zealand and the UK.

SHEILA DEWICK is the learning support co-ordinator at the Cooper Comprehensive School in Bicester, Oxfordshire. She has been a teacher for 12 years. In a former post as a community tutor she worked closely with Oxfordshire initiatives established to develop the curriculum for low-attaining pupils. In her current post, held for the last three years, she has worked towards establishing a cross-curricular collaborative role in line with a 'whole school' policy approach.

ROY HOWARTH was born in Sheffield and attended Wimbledon Art College where he qualified in fine art as a sculptor. He then taught in a London comprehensive school before moving to Beechcroft School, a boarding school for secondary-aged boys with EBD, where he became deputy head. Sixteen years ago he was appointed to the headship of Northern House School in Oxford.

ANN KIBBY has been headteacher of Oughtonhead Junior School (Hitchen, Hertfordshire) for the past ten years. She has also worked in secondary, middle and primary schools, and regularly talks to groups of teaching and ancillary staff about behaviour management and special educational needs.

ROY LUND is headteacher of a special school for pupils with EBD. He is a former local authority advisor for special education, and has produced a number of publications on EBD issues.

MIKE SAMUELS is headteacher of Enborne Lodge School, Newbury, Berkshire, a post he has held for the past 18 years. After graduating from Sussex University and completing teacher training at London University he taught in Zambia for three years. He then taught in boarding schools in the independent and maintained sectors in the UK. Since 1987 he has been the chair of the Committee of Headteachers of Residential Special Schools in the South East of England.

CHAPTER 1

Introduction: The Special Curricular Needs of Children with Emotional and Behavioural Difficulties

By Paul Cooper

This book addresses the question: what practical measures can be taken to maximise access to the formal school curriculum for pupils who have emotional and behavioural difficulties (referred to as EBD)? The chapters in this book deal with some of the answers that have been found to this question by educators working in a variety of educational settings for children of school age who exhibit EBD.

This is intended to be a practical book that focuses on the day-to-day experience of educators as *they themselves* describe it. The book should, therefore, be useful to people working with pupils with EBD who are seeking insight into this issue. The book can be used as a source of ideas that might be tried out in the school and classroom, and as a basis for reflection on and discussion of current practice.

These writers do not present themselves as lofty experts, though they are all well respected by informed colleagues in their fields. They demonstrate in their writing, however, that they have much to say that will be of practical interest to teachers, about their ways of approaching the everyday problems of teaching the formal curriculum to children exhibiting emotional and behavioural difficulties.

By way of introduction, a brief account will be given of some of the key issues that are faced by those teaching pupils with EBD and that relate to the ideas and practices described in the rest of the book.

Emotional and Behavioural Difficulties in Schools

The history of emotional and behavioural difficulties in British schools is marked by changes in the degree to which schools have taken responsibility for the treatment and alleviation of such difficulties. Whereas the earliest definitions of 'maladjustment' defined the difficulties entirely in terms of individual pathology, the 1960s, 1970s and 1980s saw the increasing dominance of the view that EBD is a form of socially constructed deviance (Laslett, 1983; Hargreaves et al., 1975). The key idea here is that behaviour is not good or bad in and of itself. Behaviour is determined good or bad by the observer of the behaviour, in accordance with the observer's values and expectations. It follows from this that if we are to understand fully the nature of EBD we must pay close attention to these very values and expectations.

The outcomes of various research studies have repeatedly and convincingly suggested to us that instances of EBD in schools may often be related to the nature of such values and expectations (Mortimore et al., 1988; Schostak, 1983; Reynolds and Sullivan, 1979; Rutter et al., 1979; Hargreaves et al, 1975; Sharp and Green, 1975), with the implication that these problems are often most effectively dealt with by changing these values and expectations, rather than by changing the individual child (Cooper, 1993; Cronk, 1987).

Standing on a threshold

Having said the above, it should be noted that at the time of writing we stand in Britain at what may be the threshold of a shift back towards more individualised explanations of EBD. It may well be the case that we have often overstated the institutional effects and paid insufficient attention to the importance of individual factors, in seeking explanations for and responses to EBD in schools (see Norwich, 1990).

Recent research from the USA and Europe suggests that between 30 per cent and 50 per cent of children displaying aggressive and antisocial behaviour have an associated problem known as Attention Deficit Hyperactivity Disorder (ADHD) in which organic problems are implicated. Similarly, problems of a more internalising nature (i.e. neuroticism), referred to as Attention Deficit Disorder (i.e. without hyperactivity), have been found to be associated with organic differences (Hinshaw, 1994; Barkley, 1990). Current estimates suggest that between 3 per cent and 5 per cent of school-aged children in the USA have this disorder. If similar proportions are reported in Britain, we may well find an increased demand for the drug and individualised treatments that are favoured in the USA by clinicians treating this condition.

We cannot, at the present time, know what the impact of ADHD will be on British education. We can, however, confidently assert that, whatever the outcome, the nature of the school environment will continue to play a significant role in the prevention of the development of EBD and in its control and alleviation. This is because whether a child's EBD is caused by inappropriate schooling, social deprivation, parental incompetence, family dysfunction or organic differences, the degree to which these difficulties interfere with the child's access to effective learning experiences will be considerably influenced by the school environment.

Emotional and Behavioural Difficulties and the School Environment

The school environment can be seen to play a major role in the learning process. It is in fact a major vehicle for the delivery of the 'hidden curriculum'. It is through their interactions with the school environment that pupils learn about the values of the school. They learn about what is and is not valued; who is and who is not valued. They also learn how to value themselves. Where schools are punitive and coercive in their treatment of pupils, pupils themselves tend to adopt similar styles of behaviour (Schostak, 1983; Reynolds and Sullivan, 1979). Where schools are rigid in their academic labelling of pupils, pupils tend to fall into polarised groups: those who are successful and who, therefore, gain self-esteem from the school experience, against those who are the failures and who find school a source of rejection and humiliation. The former develop pro-school values and attitudes, while the latter are likely to reject school and form anti-school subcultures (Hargreaves, 1967).

The school environment, therefore, plays a key role in the development and alleviation of EBD. Where a child has difficulties that originate outside the school, the school can be a place where those difficulties are either magnified or, in some sense, compensated for. One successful comprehensive school headteacher has described her school as a 'sanctuary' for pupils coming from aversive home backgrounds (Cooper, 1993). She goes on to say:

'You've got to have children wanting to come to school, no matter how bad things are at home, or no matter how unsuccessful they feel in being taught. You've got to entice them to school, and let them see school as a way forward; an enjoyable place to be; something they're going to get something out of.'

(Cooper, 1993, p.192)

In order to achieve these aspirations, the structures of schooling have to be designed with a view to their *educational* effects. Schools have to ask themselves three major questions:

3

1. What are the values that we ought to be teaching our pupils?
2. What values are we actually teaching our pupils?
3. How can we ensure that our school is organised to reinforce the values we believe to be positive, and challenge those we believe to be negative?

In the case of the school referred to in the previous paragraph, answers to these questions produced the following reforms in key structures of the school:

- the development of a discipline system that was structurally simple, and designed on the basis of minimum necessary intervention, with built-in structures for teacher support, while maintaining the pupil's right to be heard;
- the introduction of a school-wide reward structure that ensured the availability of public recognition and rewards to all pupils for a wide variety of achievements both within and outside the formal curriculum;
- the redesign of the school curriculum to offer all pupils a broad and balanced curriculum throughout the secondary phase, so as to avoid the academic/non-academic divide;
- an overhaul of curriculum delivery methods to make the curriculum accessible to the full ability range; introduction of modular courses, use of community resources; more interactive teaching styles;
- the integration of all pupils with special educational needs (SEN) (including those with EBD) and specialist staff into mainstream classes;
- the redistribution of pastoral-academic responsibilities, so that pastoral care was seen to extend to curriculum areas; making subject departments and pastoral staff aware of the relationship between teaching, learning and pupils' pastoral needs;
- the employment of a full-time school counsellor.

These measures are designed to incorporate all pupils into the school community, by giving them all opportunities for success within a structured and supportive environment.

Emotional and Behavioural Difficulties and the Curriculum

It is clear to anyone who has given thought to the subject of the school curriculum, particularly in relation to EBD pupils, that the formal curriculum is only one of many important structures within the school. The formal curriculum is in constant interaction with these other structures. There will only be equality of access to the curriculum for pupils if each of these structures is designed with such equality in mind. It is pointless, for example, having an individual curriculum geared towards the pace and developmental rate of individual pupils, if pupils are to be rewarded on a normative basis, with the child achieving the highest level of attainment receiving the most valued reward. Such a system of assessment and reward is likely to undermine the self-esteem of the children at the lower attainment levels and so depress their attainment by undermining their motivation to succeed.

For the curriculum to be accessible to *all* pupils, schools must enable *all* pupils to feel successful when they achieve progress, however small the range or slow the pace of that progress, and however that stands in relation to the progress of other pupils. Pupils must be encouraged to feel that their learning is as important as that of other pupils. It has to be noted that there is a tension between these requirements and the demands of the National Curriculum. In spite of the proposals presented in the recent Dearing Report (DfE, 1993) and the revisions to the National Curriculum (DfE, 1994), the National Curriculum still presents a number of obstacles to teaching and learning for children with SEN (see Norwich, 1993), and EBD in particular.

The division of the National Curriculum into key stages, and the eight-level assessment model, are measures designed to facilitate the kinds of normative comparisons which inevitably present SEN pupils as low achievers. The rigid time limits and the reliance on literacy skills in the Standard Assessment Tasks (SATs) similarly disadvantage pupils whose lack of confidence makes task completion slow and whose literacy skills lag behind their conceptual skills. The heavy burden of content in many of the subject areas, and the linking of programmes of study to key stages, will make it difficult for teachers to capitalise on individual students' personal interests in ways that were possible prior to the advent of the National Curriculum.

The possible range of learning

The importance of tuning in to the individual pupil's state of knowledge, and of allowing the pupil to relate to new knowledge and learning tasks in individual and even idiosyncratic ways cannot be underestimated. This is true for all pupils, but especially true for pupils with EBD. The Russian psychologist Vygotsky (1987) invented the term 'Zone of Proximal Development' (ZPD) to describe the particular learning capabilities of the individual. The ZPD represents the possible range of learning that an individual can achieve with the help of, for example, a teacher. The range is determined by the particular constellation of skills and knowledge that the child already possesses.

The role of the educator is to present new knowledge to the child in ways that enable the child to make sense of the new knowledge in terms of existing knowledge they already hold. This process of facilitation is referred to as 'scaffolding' (Bruner and Haste, 1987). The underlying message of this approach is that learning is essentially an individual and an active business. Pupils need to be given the opportunity to engage with and cognitively manipulate new knowledge in their own (sometimes very personal) ways (Barnes, 1976). The applicability of this learning theory to the everyday world of teaching and learning in mainstream secondary school has been demonstrated in recent research (Cooper and McIntyre, 1993; 1994a; 1994b).

The Importance of Differentiation

It is when we come to acknowledge the individuality of learners that we recognise the importance of differentiation in the planning of learning tasks. This is not a new idea to teachers who work with pupils with SEN. Effective differentiation depends on our knowing our pupils, and on our willingness to listen to our pupils. It is at this point that the traditional therapeutic concerns of teachers of EBD children meet the educational concerns.

Of all the forms of differentiation identified in a recent study carried out by the National Foundation for Educational Research (NFER) (Straddling and Saunders, 1993), the most important for EBD pupils is that of differentiation by 'dialogue'. This refers to the planning of tasks on the basis of active negotiation with pupils. The more we know about an individual pupil's emotional state, motivational level, and current knowledge, understanding and skills, the more successful we will be in planning educational experiences that are likely to lead to effective learning. Such a dialogue can only take place in an environment which is conducive to the promotion of pupils' self-esteem and confidence.

Care and Control

While this book does not deal directly with issues of care and control of children with EBD, this is clearly a topic of central importance to workers with such children. The key point to be made here is that the curriculum can and should contribute to the care and control processes, and that there should be an underlying consistency between the educational and care/control practices.

Focus on the individual

The way the curriculum itself is delivered is enormously important in preventing and alleviating emotional and behavioural difficulties. A key issue here in promoting academic achievement is to focus on the individual pupil. Rewards and praise are most likely to lead to increased motivation and success if they are focused on individual *progress*, rather than attainment. This is one of the ideas underlying effective differentiation. For this to happen, teachers need to create learning situations that enable pupils to extend their learning in the presence of appropriate support. Clearly, individual differences among pupils mean that for this to be done effectively, teachers need to have considerable knowledge of the individual characteristics of pupils. This is not always easy to achieve in the busy overcrowded classroom.

Fortunately, effective learning, rather like co-operative behaviour, seems to be facilitated when pupils are given a high degree of responsibility. The use of group work, self-directed learning techniques, peer tutoring, peer and self-assessment all help to create an atmosphere of co-operation and collaboration within the classroom that is also conducive to good behaviour and effective learning. Collaborative classrooms in which pupils are encouraged to be self-directing create opportunities for teachers and support staff to engage in individual and small group consultation: a process which enables staff to focus their support where it is most needed at any given time across the full range of pupils.

Collaboration

The skills of autonomy and self-direction that these experiences engender in pupils need to be equally valued when dealing with disciplinary issues. Disciplinary problems are by definition shared problems that need to be dealt with collaboratively. The 1989 Children Act makes coercive approaches to control no longer legally justifiable, and the 1994 Code of Practice (DfE, 1994b) makes such approaches incompatible with the need for pupils to be fully involved in decision making processes in the SEN context.

Consistent with certain aspects of the National Curriculum, these documents stress the need for partnership between staff and the child with SEN in developing appropriate responses to his or her needs. This highlights the value of approaches to dealing with EBD that are therapeutic and consultative, whereby the child with EBD is placed in situations where solutions to his or her problems are framed in terms of the choices that he or she makes.

Achieving the appropriate kind of incorporative school and classroom ethos on which positive behaviour often depends is not a simple matter. Such outcomes depend on an across-the-board consistency between the declared school values and the everyday realities of school life. This means that pupils need to have the sense that they are valued and important reinforced through the daily routines of school life, and in their interactions throughout the school. For this to happen, all staff need to be committed to these values.

Commitment, for staff as for pupils, follows from involvement. Thus the establishment of the school's values and the development of policies and practices that are designed to meet these values should come about through a process of consultation and collaboration which involves the whole school community - staff, pupils and governors - as well as parents. This requires open debate and self-evaluation that can only happen when these issues are made a formal priority to which time is devoted. Opportunities for open discussion, which takes in all constituencies of opinion within the school, must be created, and everyone must be made to feel that they have had some involvement in the decision making process.

Effective Curriculum Delivery

And so, we return to where we started. Effective curriculum delivery depends on the ability of the whole institution to support the individual pupil by giving him or her opportunities to develop a positive sense of self, which is the basic requirement that everyone needs to take on new challenges of the type imposed by the formal curriculum. In the following chapters indications are given of some of the ways that this challenge is being met, with regard to EBD pupils, in a variety of educational settings.

References

Barkley, R (1990) *Attention Deficit Hyperactivity Disorder: a Handbook for Diagnosis and Treatment,* Guilford: New York.

Barnes, D (1976) *From Communication to Curriculum,* Penguin: Harmondsworth.

Bruner, J and Haste, H (1987) *Making Sense: the Child's Construction of the World,* Methuen: London.

Cooper, P (1993) *Effective Schools for Disaffected Students,* Routledge: London.

Cooper, P and McIntyre, D (1993) 'Commonality in teachers' and pupils' perceptions of effective learning,' *British Journal of Educational Psychology, Vol. 63,* pp 381-399.

Cooper, P and McIntyre, D (1994a) 'Teachers' and pupils' perceptions of effective classroom learning,' in M Hughes (ed) *Perceptions of Teaching and Learning,* Multilingual Matters: Clevedon.

Cooper, P and McIntyre, D (1994b) 'Patterns of interaction between teachers' and students' classroom thinking, and their implications for the provision of learning opportunities, *Teaching and Teacher Education,* (in press).

Cronk, K (1987) *Teacher Pupil Conflict in Secondary Schools,* Falmer: Lewes.

DfE (1993) (The Dearing Report): *The National Curriculum and Its Assessment,* SCAA: London.

DfE (1994a) *The National Curriculum Orders,* DfE: London.

DfE (1994b) *The Code of Practice on the Identification and Assessment of Children with SEN,* DfE: London.

Hargreaves, D (1967) *Social Relations in a Secondary School,* RKP: London.

Hargreaves, D, Hester, F and Mellor, F (1975) *Deviance in Classrooms,* RKP: London.

Hinshaw, S (1994) *Attention Deficits and Hyperactivity in Children,* Sage: Thousand Oaks, CA.

Laslett, R (1983) *Changing Perceptions of Maladjusted Children, 1945-81,* AWMC: Portishead.

Mortimore, P, Sammons, L, Stoll, L and Ecob, R (1988) *School Matters,* Open: London.

Norwich, B (1990) *Reappraising Special Needs Education,* Cassell: London.

Norwich, B (1993) 'The National Curriculum and SEN,' in O'Hear, P and White, J (eds.) *Assessing the National Curriculum,* Paul Chapman: London.

Reynolds, D and Sullivan, M (1979) 'Bring schools back in,' in Barton, L and Meighan, R (eds.) *Schools, Pupils and Deviance,* Nafferton: Driffield.

Rutter, M, Maughan, B, Mortimore, P and Ouston, J (1979) *Fifteen Thousand Hours,* Open: London.

Schostak, J (1983) *Maladjusted Schooling,* Falmer: London.

Sharp, R and Green, A (1975) *Education and Social Control,* RKP: London.

Straddling, B and Saunders, L (1993) 'Differentiation in practice: responding to the needs of all pupils,' *Educational Research,* Vol. 35, No. 2, pp 127-137.

Vygotsky, L (1987 edn.) *The Collected Works of L S Vygotsky,* Reiber, R and Carton A (eds.) Plenum: London.

PART ONE

ENSURING CURRICULUM ENTITLEMENT FOR PUPILS WITH EMOTIONAL AND BEHAVIOURAL DIFFICULTIES IN MAINSTREAM SCHOOLS

CHAPTER 2

Pupils with Emotional and Behavioural Difficulties and the Curriculum in a Mainstream Junior School

By Ann Kibby and Tricia Beavis

Oughtonhead Junior School

Oughtonhead is a mainstream junior school sharing a site with a playgroup, and nursery and infant schools, in the small market town of Hitchin, in north Hertfordshire.

The commonly held perception of Hitchin is as an area of advantage and prosperity, but there are areas of high unemployment, social deprivation and poverty.

Many of Oughtonhead's pupils are from disadvantaged families where the parents work hard to support them in spite of their difficulties. Housing in the local area is a mixture of mature council and some private ownership. There is a higher than average proportion of children with learning difficulties because of emotional and behavioural problems. For some of the children, school is a safe, secure environment and they respond with affection and loyalty, expressing regret when term ends.

The number of children on roll is 138 organised into five classes plus a special unit for children with learning difficulties because of emotional and behavioural problems. The children on the roll of the unit are statemented under the 1981 Education Act and there may be a maximum of eight. Those children are placed by County Hall (following advice from all professional agencies) having been referred from other schools in Hitchin and surrounding villages.

The staff

Staff employed by the school totals 27, which includes teachers, welfare assistants, midday supervisory assistants, caretaker and cleaners.

There have been many changes in staffing over the last eight years, including temporary appointments, but the nucleus of staff has remained stable, working collaboratively with a flexible and sensitive approach. As far as is possible, we have been able to appoint a mature but enthusiastic staff who present a united front when working with the children. The special unit is staffed by a teacher in charge and a full-time welfare assistant and is considered an integral feature of the school.

The governing body is representative of the locality, having the interests of the residents at heart. It is totally supportive of the community, parents and staff, offering appropriate advice and assistance where necessary.

Parent involvement

There has been improved attendance at school functions, in particular parents consultation evenings and curriculum events. Participation in fundraising offers parents the opportunity to support the school, while there is a reluctance to be involved in the organisation. A proportion of parents find it difficult to help at home with reading, tables, spellings and so forth.

Cross-phase liaison is developing, creating effective links with the infant and secondary schools.

Regular meetings to consider both pastoral, administrative and curriculum matters are a feature of our school development plan.

School history

Historically, the school opened in the mid-1960s drawing 240 children from what was then a densely populated area of young families. In the early 1970s, a special unit was added to cater for children with learning difficulties in the area. By the mid-1970s, four mobile classrooms were added and the school was full to the brim. Parents had raised money for the swimming pool which is still in use today.

In the late 1970s, the school roll plummeted as part of the national trend, which was further exacerbated by the development of a private housing estate which included a new open plan school.

Meeting the Needs

A decade ago it was felt by some of the existing staff that two problems needed addressing:

- behaviour around the school was inappropriate (a nucleus of children being very noisy, defiant and disobedient);
- the curriculum was not felt by the children to be relevant (evident in the poor achievement and presentation of work, stress among teachers).

The following action evolved:

1. Visits were made to schools where it was evident that good practice was taking place.
2. Advice was sought from county officers and advisers about the needs of individual children and staffing levels which had recently been cut.
3. Discussions were held with staff concerning the need for appropriate access to the curriculum.
4. An environmental topic was planned which involved the whole school.

It was decided to adopt three specific aims:

- to build better relationships between children;
- to build better relationships with the adults around them;
- to build a better relationship with the natural world and their own environment.

Outcomes from this early action were positive. We found that far more discussion took place between the staff and children. Staff began to work more collaboratively, sharing ideas and resources. There was an improved attitude to work and examples of good behaviour could be seen in some classes. Children began to respect each other and care for school and individual property.

Interestingly, there was also a significant changeover of teaching staff which initially left the school slightly unstable. This allowed for increased flexibility when appointing new staff.

From these very humble beginnings began the long and winding road to our present philosophy and practice.

Special Unit for Children with EBD

Soon after the 1981 Education Act, it was noticeable that the nature of provision for the special unit for pupils with EBD had to become more specific and accountable as this was considered a valuable and expensive resource.

Specific aims and guidelines were laid down by the county, the main aim being to integrate the children with EBD back into the mainstream.

The teacher in charge of the unit was to be responsible for implementing the integration, but in collaboration with the mainstream class teacher.

This had implications for the teaching staff, particularly those accepting children with EBD into the mainstream. One consequence was an increase in dialogue between teachers, extending their skills in managing children with behavioural difficulties, not just those in the special unit. Newly appointed staff are made aware at interview of the SEN needs of both mainstream and unit children with the expectation that they will have to meet these children's needs.

Teaching Approaches

We have found that in trying to help all children gain access to the formal curriculum, we had to first home in on the informal and social aspects of school life and develop strategies to enhance the self-esteem of children with EBD in the mainstream.

We began to devise a whole school policy for encouraging good behaviour alongside our curriculum policies.

Adults

We have supported staff to cope with inappropriate behaviour while trying to avoid confrontation. Dialogue is encouraged and deliberately initiated between all adults involved in the school community. We emphasise the need for adults to be positive and praise the children, highlighting courteous behaviour by example and discussion.

We try to be aware of the use of language, emphasising the positive. Through assemblies, we try to develop the children's spiritual, moral and citizenship education. Collaborative teaching has become beneficial rather than the removal of groups of children from class (although obviously this is not always appropriate).

Staff are encouraged to greet all visitors with warmth and sensitivity as part of our welcoming, open-door policy to parents.

Children

Children were involved in drawing up class and school codes of conduct. We asked them to tell us the kind of behaviour they liked and disliked. We regularly talk

16

to the children and keep a watchful eye for rough play, which we discourage. Children are made aware that the adults in the school talk to each other and follow up instances of bad behaviour. We encourage friendly, positive play providing equipment such as small balls, quoits, ropes and so on. We have designated an area for talking and quiet play.

We have tried to encourage teachers to value the importance of routines for entering class at the beginning of sessions. Where appropriate, behaviour books, charts and contracts are drawn up, recording the positive and indicating room for improvement.

Strategies to Help Staff Cope
The value of communication
We believe that all caring teachers have the ability to acquire skills in managing the behaviour of children with emotional difficulties. It is essential to develop a supportive atmosphere where staff feel confident to approach others and discuss children experiencing particular difficulties.

Underlying our approach to working with EBD children in the mainstream is a belief in the value of communication.

Staff are made aware of when parents or children need extra-sensitive care. This may take place informally or during discussions at staff meetings. It has become accepted practice that teachers have dialogue with parents at the end of the day. The frequency is decided between teacher and parent and may change according to need. Positive comments are encouraged.

Classroom strategies
Difficulties do arise when children are working, but good practice can contribute to the maintenance of a calm, pleasant atmosphere.

Prevention
There are many factors evident in our classrooms which help minimise disruption:

- effective positioning of the teacher according to the type of lesson in progress, e.g. moving about the room during practical lessons, or sitting during silent reading as an example of personal enjoyment;
- sensitive composition of groups allowing for personality differences;
- removal of temptation, as in 'shall I look after that for you?';
- positive support for staff, and encouragement to seek help in time;

- drawing attention to children's success, which might involve asking them what they are good at, and the continuous use of award books to celebrate achievement;
- giving the children the opportunity to explain their feelings and actions and the knowledge that matters will be sorted out;
- praising appropriate behaviour, either to another adult in the child's hearing or to the class, without causing disruption;
- use of non-verbal communication, e.g. smile, a warning look, hand on the shoulder, taking a child by the hand, and gestures which show warmth;
- enormous attempts to maintain a sense of humour and of proportion.

Effective action

In order to resolve difficulties with the minimum of disruption, teachers employ many strategies to gain co-operation:

- refusing to be drawn into a confrontation, if necessary waiting until calm is restored;
- avoiding sarcasm and negative comments about the person - it is preferable to criticise the deed, not the child;
- diverting attention from potential confrontation by offering a choice, sending on a message, changing the task, focusing on the work;
- enabling children to have a way out, so as not to lose face;
- refraining from making hasty judgements;
- delaying intervention when considered appropriate.

Summary

On reflection, our whole school approach seems to have enabled the adults in the school to develop a trust and confidence in their own skills to manage children with EBD in the mainstream. This situation has evolved through individual staff development, formal inservice training (INSET), stability of teaching staff and positive leadership.

Recording Children's Achievement

Our school policy aims to enhance children's self-esteem. We do this by celebrating achievement in all aspects of school life.

Award Books

Each child is given an award book on entering Oughtonhead, a simple exercise book in a plastic cover which accompanies the child through the school and becomes their property when they leave. All adults working in school record success in:

- learning;
- behaviour;

- manners;
- helpfulness;
- performance;
- attitude.

Teachers are reminded to check that all children receive at least one award each half term. Each time a comment is recorded, the child's book is taken to the office to have a sticker added.

We use a wide range of commercially produced attractive self-adhesive stickers. These highlight some of the following:

16.10	Miles is trying really hard today to do the right thing. S. M.	
17.10	For beautiful singing at our 'Harvest' assembly. S. M.	
16.11	For very good contribution to discussion about the 'Witches of Pendle' this morning. S. M.	
25.11	For doing a lovely job for me. Washed class globe beautifully. S. M.	
2.12	For remaining in his seat and working well. S. M.	

The award books are highly valued by both children and parents who have access to them at consultation evenings.

Individual Approaches

If, in spite of all our support and encouragement, there are children who do not respond, we make a special arrangement. We try to build a relationship in which the child learns to:

- trust an adult;
- explain the source of difficulty, openly and honestly;
- clarify the facts;
- establish cause and effect;
- consider the course of events;
- plan for the future.

Sometimes there needs to be a formal record made. This would take the form of a chart or written contract, the purpose of which must be understood by the child, with opportunity for reward when success is achieved.

We have tried the following:

- contracts - child/child
    - child/adult
    - group;
- class Code of Conduct;
- daily behaviour books or cards;
- smile charts;
- daily worksheets with tasks listed by the teacher;
- team points to encourage co-operation.

Contracts and charts have more meaning when the child is involved in the content and able to contribute ideas, signing as an equal partner.

Summary

We feel strongly that it is important to have a whole school approach which allows children to achieve as individuals. This should lead to enhanced self-esteem, greater confidence and a more responsible approach to their own learning.

This forms the basis of our approach to the formal curriculum.

Nature of the Curriculum

To quote from the Elton Report 1989 (HMSO):
'All parties involved in the planning, delivery and evaluation of the curriculum

should recognise the quality of the content and the teaching and learning methods through which it is delivered are important influences on pupils' behaviour.'

We have found that the criteria mentioned in the above statement are particularly applicable to meeting the needs of our children. Careful consideration is given to a whole school approach which determines the organisation of children, staff and resources as well as the curriculum.

An inspector (HMI) commented earlier this year that we had built up tremendous strength in the staff as we had encouraged change of role and opportunity for staff. These have included the following changes in areas of responsibility:

- part-time to full-time;
- supply teacher to class teacher;
- class teacher to part-time;
- mainstream teacher to unit;
- deputy head to acting-headship in another school;
- special unit teacher to acting-deputy headship;
- discretionary allowances for special projects, e.g. induction of staff.

We consider it important to arrange classes with the following in mind:

- date of birth order which restricts age range in each class;
- positive friendship groups encouraged;
- separation of children where appropriate;
- ethnic mix;
- mixed ability;
- previous teacher;
- gender;
- parental wishes (only if absolutely essential);
- smaller classes for the younger children to enable a positive start in school;
- consultation with the infant school on pastoral care, e.g. groupings of children.

Resources
Libraries
The libraries have been developed as a focus, helping to create the right atmosphere as children and adults enter the school building. We are fortunate in

having considerable space, which we have used to advantage. The children have free access to any of our library areas:

* fiction;
* non-fiction;
* share-reading;
* scheme books.

In addition, there are resources areas for science, maths, humanities, music, art and multi-cultural education, all of which are easily accessible to adults and children.

Display areas

Creating the right environment has involved display areas in corridors and hall, allowing space for three-dimensional work. This includes work designed by children, relevant artifacts from museums, art loans or other resources. Great emphasis is placed on children and staff valuing work by all groups of society and considerable informal discussion takes place.

Classrooms

We are building up a wide range of equipment in each class, such as:

* dictionaries;
* maths equipment and books;
* language books;
* library trolleys.

We are fortunate in having large classrooms which incorporate room for cloakroom, toilets, practical and discussion areas, together with the normal seating arrangement found in all classrooms.

An exception to this is a small classroom where we usually base the older children. They have split facilities, which enables the class to overflow using adjacent areas and main toilet and cloakroom. This is not ideal but we feel it encourages them to be more responsible for their own behaviour and learning.

Class teachers organise their own room to include:

* library area - trolleys for class selection of library books;
* carpet area for discussion or informal activities;
* practical area - includes sinks and tables;

- display areas - 2D and 3D;
- cupboards and work tops providing easy access for the children;
- everyday items accessible on each block of tables, e.g. pots of coloured pencils, erasers and rulers;
- easy visibility of the blackboard.

National Curriculum
Planning

When planning our work, all teachers use the National Curriculum documents as the focus. Throughout the year we endeavour to cover all areas of the curriculum, aiming for breadth, balance, relevance and differentiation.

We now have a four-year topic cycle, each class covering the topics allocated for the year. It has become essential to plan the work carefully, and this can involve advisory teachers, head, subject co-ordinators as well as class and support teachers.

Topics for 1993/94 were as follows:

Birds of prey	Water
Space	Structures
Electricity and magnetism	Invaders and settlers
Locality (geography-based)	

Cross-curricular links

Where possible, we recognise the cross-curricular links but we have realised increasingly that some areas of the curriculum have to be autonomous. In maths it would be appropriate to link capacity with water, but many areas of maths, such as algebra, need covering separately.

In general, our children are stimulated and excited by the rich variety of topics now covered in school. The themes allow for differences of gender and cultural background.

To create added interest, we plan the following to link in with the area under study:

- visits to places, e.g. museums, libraries, the common, theatre, the local environment;
- visitors to school, e.g. birds of prey, brass ensemble, theatre groups, science shows;

- visitors to school who highlight health and safety, e.g. local police, railway police, road safety, dental hygiene, physical fitness and leisure activities;
- visitors from the community, e.g. governors, community centre (including youth club), senior citizens, parents with special skills.

Content of the curriculum

It has been apparent for a long time that the National Curriculum is overloaded with content. Nevertheless, we have endeavoured to cover all the subject areas including RE as part of our broad and balanced curriculum (this pre-dates the National Curriculum). We are presenting more topics but feel that some children's knowledge lacks depth, although they are learning a greater variety of skills, there is more progression and a better use of resources.

We have readily accepted the National Curriculum and attempt to cover the content to the best of our ability.

Ensuring breadth, balance, relevance and differentiation
Breadth

This involves the four-year topic cycle mentioned above. The underlying principles in our planning aim to ensure that the child develops as a whole. Opportunities are given for spiritual and moral, aesthetic and creative, human, social and physical development as well as the accepted academic curriculum.

We monitor and review regularly statements of attainment covered to allow for depth of understanding or, in other cases, to avoid repetition.

Balance

We recognise the need to offer a balance between the following methods of teaching:

- individual;
- group;
- whole class.

Whole-class teaching has become more valued as a means of introducing an area of study such as mathematics, topic.

It is usual practice to find only one area of the curriculum being taught at a given time in individual classrooms.

Grouping within a class can take place on a social or ability basis according to the needs of the children or area of curriculum being taught.

Allowances are made for individuals in need of additional support or one-to-one tuition which may involve withdrawal but usually happens within the classroom.

We are aware of the need to provide children with a curriculum that is rich and varied. We try to ensure the children have opportunities for:

discussion	observation
investigating	reporting
working together	problem solving
researching	writing, drawing
reading	displaying.

It will be obvious that this list is not comprehensive owing to the complexities of the teaching/learning situation.

Relevance

Children at Oughtonhead Junior School are readily involved in thematic work, but some are disadvantaged due to limited experience of the wider world which stems from their home environment. Resources from home are not always readily available but the children seem to appreciate efforts made by staff to provide items of interest and relevance. One example was when we borrowed display cases of stuffed birds of prey to link with this term's red-tail falconry demonstration and follow-up work.

Not all topics under the National Curriculum are readily relevant to the lives of the children. Nevertheless, the enthusiasm of staff and children can compensate.

The use of information technology (IT), and LOGO in particular, features in all classes, the children probably enjoying LOGO work more than the staff.

This, together with the introduction of a new scheme in maths, has enhanced the learning possibilities. The children are positive in their approach to mathematics.

Word processing was initiated through funding, for children with emotional and behavioural difficulties. The hardware and training was funded by a government grant. This gave opportunities for mainstream children with special needs to develop IT capabilities. Further training was accepted by two mainstream teachers who started up word processing and data handling with their own class.

Differentiation

Because of the nature of a proportion of the children, teachers are often faced with the challenge of changing approach and/or materials in order to meet the children's needs in lessons. This requires a degree of flexibility in order to adapt to the prevailing mood and to respond sensitively and inventively. Tasks may also need to be modified or postponed.

This can be disadvantageous when trying to fulfil the requirements of the National Curriculum.

We do have similar expectations of children but we make allowances for individual needs according to the level of ability, concentration and degree of emotional instability. All children are expected to acquire a core of knowledge, concepts, skills and attitudes.

Progression and continuity

Our present methods of planning are more likely to provide progression and continuity. Stability of staff contributes to a common approach in rewarding children for their achievements, however small. All members of staff interact positively with children from all classes and we operate a policy that encourages teachers to promote good behaviour by dealing with any misbehaviour they encounter anywhere in the school.

Creating an Environment of Respect

We aim to provide a secure environment where we value all children equally. We make efforts to develop the following qualities.

Responsibility

Children are encouraged to understand that they are learning for themselves. They are also expected to accept responsibility for their wrongdoings, their part in them and the possible effects.

Self-respect and respecting others

We promote the idea that being different adds richness to our lives and it is important that teachers show this in the way they talk to children. We all have a contribution to make which is equally valued.

Success and independence

It is very important that children have frequent opportunity to achieve success which is then recognised by teachers, peers, ancillaries and parents.

Children's attempts at work are valued. They need to understand that making mistakes is a natural process of learning. The significance of teachers admitting to being in the wrong should not be overlooked.

Throughout the Junior School, we are aiming to develop children's ability to:

* apply skills and concepts;
* make informed choices;
* achieve and complete tasks.

Achieving independence of learning is a long process and we recognise that children can only manage this at their own pace.

Constant encouragement and guidance is required from the teacher and we must recognise that children with learning difficulties can acquire self-motivation.

Maintaining a Positive Attitude Towards Children with Emotional and Behavioural Difficulties

To maintain a positive attitude is not easy. Working with children who have emotional difficulties is stressful, tiring and can be very demoralising, particularly when there appears to be little change for the better. The following factors have some significance on the way staff cope.

On reflection, it would appear that the hiding of difficulties by members of staff can and often does lead to problems escalating. It may also leave other staff feeling unsupported and this in turn can contribute to people feeling demoralised.

We are a small staff, reasonably united in our approach to the children. We work together on topics, share ideas and are generally open about difficulties encountered in class and around the school.

On occasions when children and teachers are under particular stress, we try to operate flexibility. This can mean diverting support staff, where they can be most useful, usually in the classroom of the child who is experiencing particular difficulties.

It helps also to approach each day as a new beginning. The children come to school having moved from the happenings of the previous day, and an acceptance of this can lead to reduced levels of stress.

Frequently, staff meet informally to discuss ways of moving children forward. This can be a very valuable time in the school day.

Maintaining a sense of proportion and humour, frequent laughter and a steady supply of treats all contribute to the maintenance of a happy staff. (Treats tend to come in the form of biscuits, cakes, chocolates, wine and so forth.)

Creating a secure classroom environment where children and adults are aware of simple routines can contribute to a calm atmosphere. Being constantly on the alert and intervening early can help prevent problems escalating.

Finding behaviour worthy of praise may sometimes be difficult, but looking for evidence, however small, can contribute to helping children feel they are achieving success.

Communication Between Parents and School
Parental involvement
We encourage working together with parents. Parents' involvement in their child's education does ensure greater success.

We do our best to keep parents informed in a variety of ways:

- letters about events and school routine;
- informal consultation with staff, e.g. popping in at the end of the school day;
- parents' evenings - formal consultation;
- open school;
- home visits by staff and headteacher;
- parents' visits to the school;
- the school award system;
- Record of Achievement;
- special events, e.g. concerts;
- parent-governors;
- voluntary work in school - in classroom work, in curriculum work, e.g. shared reading, homework, science;
- parents invited in for private appointments, e.g. starting school, when child is in trouble;
- parents invited in to meetings through an interpreter;
- formulated school policy documents available for perusal;
- contact through other professionals, e.g. educational welfare officer (EWO), school nurse;
- fundraising events.

Evidence of Success
Statistical evidence

Ways in which we measure success vary from establishing eye contact to enabling children to cope in a mainstream or moderate learning difficulties (MLD) secondary school.

Taking into account the number of SEN pupils in Oughtonhead Junior School, we feel we have been reasonably successful in the following ways:

* in the last five years, only one pupil has transferred to a unit;
* at present, only one pupil in the mainstream has a statement of special needs;
* two pupils during the past few years have been statemented for EBD provision at secondary level;
* three pupils have successfully transferred to our mainstream from EBD provision elsewhere, at infant level;
* one of these pupils at the end of Year 7 was transferred from a local secondary school to EBD provision;
* seven children from our unit have fully re-integrated in our mainstream junior and progressed to secondary level;
* three children have been recommended placement in our mainstream at the request of parents, social services and educational psychologist;
* four children have gone on to MLD secondary provision, two of whom have emotional problems;
* one child who was statemented at infant level has been successful in mainstream junior and secondary.

Case study: Jeremy

Jeremy was first referred for assessment as a top infant because of disruptive and difficult behaviour in school. He is one of five children. Jeremy needed more attention at home than his siblings and he had difficulty playing properly, being easily annoyed.

He is a healthy, active boy but has a long-standing history of ear infections and hearing difficulties and has a problem in one eye. He has had speech therapy and undergone operations on his problem eye. He has also attended weekly sessions with a Family and Child Guidance therapist. He no longer attends any form of therapy but his eye continues to give problems and he often covers it while reading.

Jeremy's statement

The statement from his previous primary school indicated some extreme uncontrolled behaviour from Jeremy. On the days he was very excitable and unable to settle to work, he would scribble on and tear up his books, torment his peers, taking their possessions and so on. He seemed unable to respond to normal discipline, jumping on furniture and running around the school. He was often a danger to himself and others at playtimes and during PE, because of deliberately running into and knocking other children over. At times, he had been aggressive to his teacher and unco-operative to her requests. When assessed, he appeared to have no particular learning difficulties, had a good general ability and a reasonable grasp of basic literacy and numeracy.

Both Jeremy's parents were concerned about his behaviour at school, regularly attended for discussions and were committed to ensuring Jeremy had any available help to overcome his problems.

The first month

Jeremy entered our unit at the beginning of his Year 4. He had turned eight the previous Easter and been out of school since the end of May. During his first month with us, Jeremy showed signs of anxiety and an over-reliance on adult support when working. He was on occasions easily upset, responded rudely when enquiries were made and exhibited very low self-esteem. He would refuse to carry out work in books or on paper.

On one occasion Jeremy folded his drawing paper into a dart and threw it, later admitting it was because he did not want to draw. When questioned about his involvement in instances of bad behaviour, Jeremy's usual response was denial of responsibility, with very poor use of eye contact, and his speech became rather clipped and aggressive. He was unable to accept the importance of honest communication and wanted to hide the truth, particularly from his mother.

By the beginning of October Jeremy's behaviour in class was more settled. He began spending more time in his mainstream class, behaving co-operatively, and he completed set tasks quickly and accurately. He had also joined the football squad and had been selected to play for the school B team.

At the end of his first year with us, Jeremy had become increasingly co-operative, responding politely to adults. He showed signs of developing patience and tolerance when involved in group activities.

Integration

Integration was increased further for Jeremy in Year 5 and he spent only Monday morning and Friday afternoon in the unit, with further time available should he request it — something he did on several occasions when finding it difficult to manage in his mainstream class. During all of this time, the class teacher and unit teacher were in regular communication, with unit support available for Jeremy and his mainstream teacher.

Now he is in Year 6, Jeremy is fully integrated in the mainstream, has no particular academic difficulty and generally conforms in class. Behaviour when unsupervised is not yet satisfactory, particularly during lunch times. Jeremy is still supported by the unit staff and if, in spite of warnings, he is beginning to play aggressively, there are still times when we keep him inside until staff are available to supervise him on the playgrounds. However, when required, Jeremy is capable of calmly explaining his involvement in an incident of bad behaviour and accepting responsibility.

At the outset, clearly defined boundaries of behaviour were explained to Jeremy and these have been enforced calmly and consistently. He has also benefited from the award book system that was in operation when Jeremy joined us, whereby he has received recognition and praise for many efforts he made to improve his behaviour.

Furthermore, we have maintained regular contact with the home. Both parents have commented on occasions that the atmosphere was improving, although Jeremy still at times behaves in a potentially dangerous manner when not allowed his own way.

Non-statemented EBD children in the mainstream
In our professional judgement, we have seven children in our mainstream who would benefit from a statement for emotional and behavioural needs. This precious resource is denied them because of one or more of the following:

- reluctance on the part of parents;
- insufficient time available from learning support services, e.g. educational psychologist;
- insufficient support from other agencies, e.g. social services;
- delayed intervention by external agencies;
- limited resources at county level to support the statementing process;
- the high level of professional skill of our mainstream and unit staff in dealing with extremes of behaviour, from the distressed introvert to the violent aggressive pupil.

Some of the unit children who needed further provision when transferring at secondary level fell into the following categories:

- Three children entered our unit during their fifth year. Because of their difficulties, this was insufficient time to meet their needs and modify their behaviour. These children went on the EBD boarding provision.

- One child had learning difficulties and went on the MLD provision.
- Another child had serious emotional problems and went to an out-of-county boarding placement.

Children's attitudes

While working towards the whole-school approach to behaviour, the atmosphere has become calmer and we have noticed the following improvements:

- children are more able to accept rules and apply them in different contexts;
- children can discuss, accept and admit personal involvement in wrongdoing;
- children are more willing to accept authority and to co-operate;
- responses to adults in charge are more positive;
- children initiate conversations with adults and many greet in a friendly, open manner;
- children can relate to staff and show interest in adults as people;
- voice and body movements are more controlled and there is better eye contact;
- most of our children are now wearing school uniform willingly;
- unit children are welcomed in mainstream classes by teachers and pupils.

We see the following qualities and behaviour in the children:

- enhanced self-esteem;
- gradual improvement in presentation of work and involvement in learning;
- more positive attitude to books and enjoyment of quiet reading time;
- more appropriate behaviour generally and less overt attention seeking;
- more awareness of one's actions on others;
- reluctance often expressed when term ends;
- regular attendance at school.

Parents' attitudes

In all our dealings with parents, we have aimed to build up an atmosphere of trust and mutual understanding, with the following benefits:

- better attendance at Parents' Consultation Evenings, across the cultures;
- more frequent visits to school by parents;
- fewer home visits carried out;
- positive comments (including compliments from parents whose children transfer from other schools) concerning the care we take over our pupils;
- improved notification of children's absences and medical requirements;
- communication of happenings in the locality.

The school environment

Our efforts to improve the environment have been rewarded by:

- seeing more care taken of property and displays (both 2D and 3D);
- desks not scribbled on;
- lack of vandalism on school site;
- library being used regularly and treated with respect.

Other successes

Lunch-time and after school clubs are extremely well attended. Children settle more readily to afternoon lessons, possibly because we took two decisions:

- no football on the hard surface of the playground;
- a quiet reading session timetabled for all at the beginning of afternoon school.

The educational psychologist attached to our school has made favourable comments to the effect that some of our children with learning difficulties are achieving their potential.

Future Developments

We recognise the close link between achieving success in the formal curriculum and the nurturing of self-esteem in children with EBD.

Building good relationships with these children is one of the key aspects in helping them feel better about themselves. Although much of this is done informally, some formal training will be required.

INSET induction

As part of our School Development, we plan to highlight INSET related to good behaviour management and to provide training for all adults working with children in our school.

Parents

One of our teachers will be inducted in order to run an 'Effective Parenting' programme, aimed at helping families with issues such as:

- discipline;
- leisure;
- stress in the family;

- playground problems;
- bullying;
- starting school.

Midday supervisory/welfare assistants
Further training will be required for MSAs on dealing confidently and effectively with children's lunch-time behaviour.

Teaching staff
We have in mind the development of cross-phase liaison, particularly in the fields of pastoral care and agreement trialing for assessment purposes. We will continue to induct new members of staff in our ways of supporting children in pastoral care and behaviour management.

Future INSET for teaching staff is to include:

- 'Keeping children safe';
- word processing and data handling;
- working with parents;
- stress management;
- regular input by advisory teachers on the creative arts to highlight the practical aspects of the curriculum;
- moral development of the children through discussion/drama on subjects such as
  - community/environment
  - friendship
  - respecting differences
  - rules and property
  as part of our involvement with the Citizenship Foundation, Primary School Project (pilot).

Implications for children
We would like to create an environment where children can pursue more purposeful play. This will entail improving playground facilities and providing equipment for use during playtimes.

To enable the children to present work of which they are proud, we intend to concentrate on cursive handwriting which we hope will lead to greater fluency.

We also need to create opportunities for children to develop as more independent learners.

Links in the community

Regular meetings have been established between the school, the educational welfare officer and the school nurse. We need to extend these valuable links, to include more contact with social services and the police.

School policies

We have started to hold meetings of senior staff and link governor to formulate our policy for special educational needs. We have discussed the latest advice from the Department for Education on SEN. The whole staff is involved in the county pilot audit for non-statemented children with special needs, which we hope will recognise the need in our school for extra funding and possibly staffing.

Conclusion

We have found it possible to give access to the National Curriculum to all children in Oughtonhead Junior School. This has been achieved in a calm and caring environment for staff, children and parents.

This is, however, a long process which requires much energy and makes considerable demands on teachers' time. A consistent whole-school approach where everyone's contribution is valued would appear to be the foundation on which to build a happy school.

CHAPTER 3

Curriculum Support with Pupils with Emotional and Behavioural Difficulties in a Mainstream Comprehensive School

By Sheila Dewick

Within this chapter I give the reader a brief introduction to the Cooper School and an overview of its learning support department. Having established the entitlement of all pupils to a broad and balanced curriculum as laid down by the 1988 Education Reform Act, I will describe problems arising from the assessment procedures and lack of flexibility in the curriculum which affect pupils with special educational needs, especially those pupils considered to exhibit emotional and behavioural difficulties. Through case studies of three pupils, I will describe the strategies used to encourage individuals to work in the GCSE options available within the school and briefly describe future developments.

The Cooper School

The Cooper School is one of two secondary schools in a market town in North Oxfordshire. The school is an 11–16 comprehensive. It has strong links with its partner primaries. The primaries comprise two large town schools, one large village school in the location of an army base and four village schools.

There are a variety of post-16 opportunities. The other secondary school in the area offers sixth form courses. Banbury and Oxford have further education colleges offering a vast range of academic and vocational courses.

Cooper School offers its pupils a friendly, purposeful atmosphere in which to study and a variety of enriching activities to support and extend their educational experience.

Learning Support Department

The learning support department identifies pupils with special educational needs through liaison with primary staff and special needs support teachers at transfer from Year 6 (primary) to Year 7 (secondary).

The categories of special needs match those identified on the Oxfordshire Rainbow forms (the system of administration for pupils with SEN).

Categories of Special Educational Need

Six categories are:

- significant learning difficulty;
- emotional and behavioural disturbance;
- physical or sensory impairment;
- specific learning difficulty;
- learning difficulty;
- those requiring high level of support and care.

Two categories added to the transfer form by the department are:

- pupils who have made great progress, who are improving, and who will need some support, but who are close to independent working;
- the exceptionally able.

Brief details on each new intake of pupils with special educational needs are circulated to all staff. The following is an example:

> *Pupil A needs to have his confidence boosted and will need a great deal of encouragement. He has a very poor self-image. He does have great difficulties. He is able to write about 50 of the first 100 common sight vocabulary words. He cannot operate independently. He will need to have instructions broken down and given one at a time. He will require in-class support across the curriculum. He will also need to be extracted for work on basic skills. He is a talented footballer.*

> *Pupil B will need in-class support and extraction. He lacks motivation. His numeracy and literacy skills are weak. He will benefit from specific help to start a task and work being set at an appropriate level. He has a low self-image and needs to be encouraged. A great deal of work needs to be done with this pupil in order to build his confidence and self-esteem.*

> *Pupil C lacks confidence, struggles with writing. Reading really developing. Will need encouragement to work independently.*

Support
The support for these pupils is organised in a variety of ways:

- in-class support (this can be through a teacher or Learning Support Assistant or LSA);
- extraction;
- both of the above;
- spelling scheme support;
- reading scheme support;
- preparation of alternative materials.

In Key Stage 3 science, English, maths, technology and modern foreign languages, the subject areas are allocated five lessons a week. In geography and history, the allocation is three lessons a week and in RE two lessons a week.

Support can be identified within three levels.

High level of support
This indicates the pupil will receive cross-curricular support in approximately two to three lessons in each curriculum area, with the exception of creative arts and PE. The child will also be withdrawn to work on basic skills. This varies from one to four sessions per week depending on the individual. There will be extra reading sessions and spelling scheme support. The extra reading sessions take place before school and during form periods.

Medium level of support
Cross-curricular support will be as shown above. The pupil will also receive extra reading sessions and spelling scheme support.

Low level of support
Some curricular support will be given to the pupil. This could include provision of specialist equipment, enlarged worksheets, alternative materials etc. The majority of in-class support is carried out by the LSAs. However, some pupils will receive help from a support teacher.

The majority of pupils withdrawn from class will be taught by a support teacher. However, occasionally they will be supervised by an LSA.

Assessment
Those pupils causing particular concern regarding their literacy levels will be assessed individually using a variety of assessment procedures. During the spring and summer terms, consultation takes place with primary class teachers and SNASTs (Special Needs Advisory and Support Teachers) in order to collect information on pupils considered to be in the special needs range.

Transfer
During consultation, the special needs co-ordinator completes the transfer document for pupils with SEN. This document is filed in the pupils' central files and in the learning support department's record system.

Those pupils transferring further up the school bring with them records from previous schools. Parents at all stages of transfer are a very good source of information.

Pupils causing particular concern regarding their literacy levels will be assessed individually using a variety of assessment procedures.

Assessment materials used are standardised tests such as the new Macmillan Individual Reading Assessment, the Aston Index, British Picture Vocabulary tests, Young's Parallel Spelling Test and the NFER-Nelson Non-Verbal Reasoning Test. Informal testing procedures such as pieces of free writing, the checking of common words, observation in class and discussions with the pupils will also be part of the procedure. The maths department administers a test devised within the department in order to assess mathematical ability. Subject teacher assessment will also be used to inform the formulation of programmes for both literacy and numeracy development.

Outside agencies
For those pupils causing great concern, after consultation with pastoral staff, subject staff, pastoral deputy and parents, referrals will be made to relevant outside agencies.

Educational psychologist

The educational psychologist negotiates dates for visits at the beginning of each term. The Learning Support Co-ordinator (LSC) circulates the date to all relevant staff. Staff then refer pupils through the LSC who sets up the timetable for each visit.

Medical

Any pupil overseen by the learning support department where a medical concern is raised, for example eyes or ears, is referred to the school nurse. She will then arrange appointments contacting school and parents with the necessary information.

Behaviour support

The Behaviour Support Teacher (BST) is in school three times a week for five to six hours. One lesson of his or her time is given over to a liaison between the BST and the LSC. Pastoral staff refer pupils to the LSC who in turn refers to the BST. The BST will meet with pastoral staff to discuss in detail their concerns regarding specific pupils. The learning support co-ordinator organises the BST's timetable and the release of pupils from lessons.

Social services

Pastoral staff refer to social services when necessary by contacting social services directly and updating on specific pupils through multi-agency meetings.

Family/Child Guidance

Pastoral staff refer to Family/Child Guidance when necessary by contacting directly, and update through multi-agency meetings.

Educational social worker

The Educational Social Worker (ESW) attends multi-agency meetings and also meets with the deputy heads responsible for upper and lower school on a weekly basis. Any information about referrals of pupils can be given through the deputies.

Multi-agency

Multi-agency meetings take place once each half term. The deputy heads of lower and upper school attend the multi-agency meetings and refer pupils.

Hearing impaired

From September 1993 we have had a profoundly deaf pupil in Cooper School. The teacher of the deaf teaches in Cooper School for approximately ten hours each week. During that time there is a liaison period for the LSC and the teacher of the deaf to update on the pupil's progress, work with staff, comments from staff and any concerns.

Differentiation

Differentiation of materials, approaches and techniques within the curriculum is particularly important. This is a continuous task, with evaluation an on-going process. Co-operation with mainstream colleagues takes place not only in a consultative situation but by working together to develop materials wherever required. Subject departments are starting to work on preparing modules with work differentiated to meet individual needs.

This is something that will take time and has to be seen as a whole-school move. The emphasis is that with support, if necessary, the class teacher is responsible for accessing all pupils to their part of the curriculum. Differentiation is part of the current school action plan. Ways forward are discussed at the curriculum development group and whole-school, department and individual INSET is taking place.

Communication and consultation

A formal point of contact for communication to colleagues in different departments has been the setting up of a learning support group with representatives from each department area. At the moment it is a way of communicating procedures and updates on pupils, and sharing curriculum initiatives prepared for pupils in the special needs range. Department representatives bring suggestions, ideas and problems for discussion. They can consult on curriculum and teaching methods for children with SEN and when necessary secure inputs to department or year group meetings.

The group meets once every half term and one member of staff from each department (with the exception of PE) attends. The LSC convenes the meeting and carries out the necessary administration. The representatives from departments are volunteers who have an interest in special needs.

Communication with all staff is extremely important. Everyone needs to know whether pupils are behaving, are motivated to work and are happy with their achievement. Teachers are more willing to work with the learning support department to plan and develop work to enable access for all pupils to the curriculum.

The Learning Support Co-ordinator's Role

The LSC's role is developing into that of a cross-curricular and collaborative model of practice. This involves offering support to pupils and teachers in mainstream as part of a whole-school approach to SEN provision. In this model the learning support co-ordinator has a far broader and more central role, including not only assessment and teaching but also giving advice and support to class and subject teachers. The role also includes working with parents of children in the SEN range and liaising with external agencies and county support services, including the educational psychology service. The learning support co-ordinator also contributes on occasions to the inservice training of staff.

Curriculum Support

Supporting pupils with special needs in Cooper School follows a pattern of majority mainstream support with some individuals having two or three 35-minute sessions a week to work on basic skills in a one-to-one or small group situation. We feel that the improved self-esteem and interest gained by access to the wider curriculum improves pupil confidence and encourages them to attempt new work. The 'deficit' model of intensive work with pupils in areas they have great difficulty in ignores their social and emotional needs and is unlikely to be effective.

Total cross-curricular integration of all pupils would be the ideal. However, with consideration to some class sizes and the skills required for the subject, this is not always possible and withdrawal is necessary. Handled sensitively with relevant materials it offers pupils the chance to progress and is viewed positively.

Pupils from the local special school, Bardwell, link into a number of different lessons two days a week. Anyone who takes part in these lessons, staff or pupils from either site, benefits enormously. The Bardwell children learn to move about a large environment. They have the opportunity to move around fairly independently at break and lunchtime and to meet a variety of people. In the curriculum there is the opportunity to experience specialist teaching and equipment that their small school cannot always provide, as with technology.

The Cooper School pupils learn to work alongside pupils with severe learning difficulties. This raises their awareness of the problems faced by pupils with multiple disabilities. This encourages their sensitivity when communicating and sharing activities with the Bardwell pupils.

Support in class

There are many benefits for EBD pupils in a support system. With an LSA or support / teacher in class, the pupils have immediate access to an adult, if concerned about the task or being drawn into behaving negatively with other pupils. The support staff build up a relationship with their pupils and are able to read the signs should the pupil begin to behave inappropriately. Owing to their experience, the support staff can often distract the pupil and avoid a confrontational situation arising between the pupil and class teacher.

Being in class and following the curriculum is of great benefit to the pupil. The support staff will generally be able to keep the pupils on task and are a form of differentiation. Due to the knowledge the support staff have of their pupils, they are in a position to alert subject staff when problems arise. This warns staff, who will consider the information given them when dealing with the pupil. If necessary, relevant updates on the pupil's progress throughout a potentially problematic day can be fed back to the department. Alternative action can then be taken. An example of this could be withdrawing the pupil from the curriculum for a short period of time to allow a specific situation to settle.

Monitoring and communication

Monitoring of all pupils with special educational needs is an important part of the department's work which takes place weekly. Department meetings held weekly give the opportunity to discuss specific pupils and enable change and update in support programmes. Changes are also communicated to all staff involved with the pupils. Careful monitoring encourages appropriate intervention and prompts further discussions with parents and, when necessary, involvement of outside agencies.

Learning support co-ordinator

The LSC attends a number of meetings where heads of department, heads of year and senior management are represented. The groups are Curriculum Development, Pastoral Development and HODY (Heads of Department and Heads of Year). These meetings enable information to be shared, decisions made and future developments aired and discussed.

Provision for Special Educational Needs in the Curriculum

In the past, individual schools have been able to design their own curriculum. The numerous factors which influence the curriculum are almost insurmountable. At the present moment the single greatest influencing factor on school curriculum is the 1988 Education Act which has at its core the National Curriculum.

The implementation of the Education Reform Act 1988 has reaffirmed the entitlement of access to the whole curriculum for all pupils. The National Curriculum Council's Circular Number 5 and Curriculum Guidance Number 2, 'A Curriculum For All', reiterate the full support of NCC: 'For the principles of maximum participation in the National Curriculum by all pupils with SEN and for the minimal use of the exceptional arrangements which are available through sections 17 – 19 of the Education Reform Act 1989.' (This refers to exemption for pupils with statements from specific curriculum areas.)

The National Curriculum promotes a broad and balanced curriculum for all children. This is their legal entitlement and the responsibility for providing for special needs within the curriculum is on all staff (Bines 1992). 'In requiring a complete overhaul of approaches to curriculum, learning, assessment, classroom and school management, the National Curriculum would thus seem to provide a range of opportunities to develop the learning consultancy role, and to improve curriculum entitlement and provision across the whole curriculum in all schools.'

Accessibility

One of the common predominant features of mainstream curricula as regards pupils with special educational needs has been that they have not always been accessible. This has caused a variety of difficulties. Consideration of the range of skills required, especially the level of literacy, has not been taken into account when tasks are set. The conceptual and learning demands are also sometimes ignored when planning work. Pupils with SEN often end up with a 'watered down' experience rather than work organised to match their ability. The advantage they gain is being involved in a mainstream curricular experience.

There is now an emphasis for all staff to not only cater for the motivated, home-supported pupils whose educational needs are primarily cognitive and exam-orientated, but to access to the curriculum a large proportion of pupils whose needs are not just cognitive but are also social and emotional.

Ainscow (1990) suggests that there are three aspects of teaching that seem to be essential for responding successfully to pupils' individual needs:

1. Teachers have to know their pupils well in terms of their existing skills and knowledge, their interests and their previous experience.
2. Pupils have to be helped to establish a personal meaning about the tasks and activities in which they are engaged.
3. Classrooms have to be organised in ways that encourage involvement and effort.

In broad terms, effective teachers achieve these aims by emphasising purpose; variety and choice; reflection and review; flexible use of resources; and co-operative learning. All teachers need to consider this in their everyday planning.

Assessment demands

Many teachers are preparing differentiated modules of work, encouraging pupils to have confidence in themselves, teaching to enable progress for all pupils.

44

However, it is suggested that the assessment demands of the National Curriculum are divisive and damaging to vulnerable children.

The first point that needs to be considered is the effect of assessment on pupils with SEN using National Curriculum levels. When a pupil with SEN transfers from primary they could be operating around level 2 across the curriculum. This can obviously be in a range — some may be operating across levels 2 – 3, others levels 1 – 2.

In the assessment procedure for the National Curriculum across subject areas, the necessary small step-by-step progression for special needs pupils is not recognised when reporting in levels. It is quite possible for some pupils to transfer at 11 operating at levels 2 – 3 across the curriculum, make progress, but leave secondary school operating at the same levels.

National Curriculum Tests

When having to take National Curriculum Tests (NCTs), the disruption to normal timetable and the amount of time spent under examination conditions may only serve to reinforce the self-esteem and low self-image that many pupils with special needs hold of themselves. Much of the work with pupils with SEN across the curriculum is built on encouragement, with a view to pupils from an 'I can't' to an 'I can' mode. One week of NCTs may wipe out the work previously achieved with these pupils in terms of confidence.

When NCT scores are reported in a level or given as a single letter, such as a W, as has been suggested, without comment, pupils may once again be put into a situation of failure.

GCSEs

Much work in all curriculum areas goes into preparing pupils for their GCSE years. It is important that when moving from Year 9 to Year 10, pupils have confidence and are motivated to work through two very important years. Receiving NCT levels may discourage, demotivate and cause a crisis of confidence. For some pupils with a variety of problems, this could very well be the last straw in a very difficult school career. Pupils may become disaffected and any point or reason for trying will be lost.

This is particularly distressing considering the NCTs will only give teachers information that they are already aware of and take time away from the very important job of teaching to enable progress.

Within Cooper School, the curriculum on offer for Years 10 and 11 has been limited to GCSE option choices following National Curriculum Key Stage 4 criteria. The demands of these options are great and particularly difficult for all special needs pupils. One group, however, is particularly challenging: pupils with emotional and behavioural difficulties.

Support in Action

In order that you may follow the reasoning behind the support structures set up for three specific pupils, I will outline the difficulties faced by the pupils regarding the curriculum, their view of school and the view they hold of themselves.

In the senior end of the school, the curriculum consists of seven subjects in GCSE option groups. All pupils follow GCSE courses in line with National Curriculum Key Stage 4 criteria in maths, English, science, technology and social studies (RE, history, geography), a modern foreign language and a creative arts option. For some pupils a single science option plus two extra lessons of maths and two study periods with staff support provides an alternative to the double science option.

This obviously poses great difficulties for any pupils experiencing learning difficulties or a range of special educational needs. Three pupils experiencing learning and emotional and behavioural difficulties were causing many staff great concern. In the first instance two were obviously identifiable moving from Year 9 to Year 10. Throughout the first term in Year 10 another pupil became particularly obvious to many staff.

Case Studies: Three Pupils
Louise

Louise is a pupil who has a significant learning difficulty. She cannot function independently, lacking the ability to read and write fluently or work at a level beyond seven years operationally. However, Louise is perceptive and orally able to communicate her ideas in class. She generally understands the content. However, she is not interested in applying herself, and will not commit herself to her reading. She is keenly interested in the reactions from her peers. This leads to lack of self-control, poor motivation and an involvement in pursuits off task, attracting negative attention from staff.

Louise can be verbally abusive and has little idea regarding classroom conventions and expectations of behaviour. She views herself as unable to do her school work and has been particularly negative about some subjects as she can see little relevance to her future employment.

Susan

Susan has a significant learning problem. Her language development has been delayed and although she has a functional basic vocabulary, it is very difficult for her to grasp new concepts. She finds it quite difficult to work independently. Her basic skills are still in the range of seven to eight years.

Susan has found it very difficult to ignore other pupils. Her difficulties in coping with the demands of different subjects cause her to be uninterested and demotivated. She has been off task and involved in situations with other pupils, attracting negative attention from staff.

Once in trouble, Susan's behaviour deteriorates to the point that she will be openly hostile, confrontational and rude to staff and other pupils. She has a limited concentration span and has carried out very little work in school or at home. She frequently forgets PE kit resulting in non-participation in this subject area. Susan has also had a poor attendance record.

Linda

Linda has problems with reading and writing but these skills are developed enough to fall into the functional category. Linda flouts authority, distracts other pupils, has been rarely on task, and is consistently loud, immature and confrontational. Linda has a very poor attendance record. She is consistently in trouble for rudeness to the staff and refusing to carry out work set.

Linda has no self-control and in practical areas can be so undisciplined that she is a risk to herself and others. Like Susan, Linda rarely brings PE kit and in the majority of lessons does not participate.

Punishments received and sanctions used

All three pupils in their lower school experience have regularly been on report card, with daily monitoring by the year head.

All three pupils have consistently gained concerns from most staff regarding their effort and behaviour in lessons when overviews are requested throughout the school year. These generally occur termly. Two pupils, Susan and Linda, have on a number of occasions been visited by the Educational Social Worker regarding their attendance. The pupils have all been categorised by pastoral staff as 'behaviorably difficult'. All three pupils have been internally and externally suspended for verbal abuse of staff and inappropriate behaviour towards other pupils and staff. Louise and Susan have statements of special educational needs.

Senior school

Susan and Louise each had five hours learning support assistant time funded by the county as a result of their statements when they transferred from the lower school. Both pupils were a great concern for all staff. Their limited skills and inappropriate behaviour led staff to believe that it would only be a matter of weeks before major incidents would require alternative provision. What that might mean, nobody knew.

Due to negotiations throughout the 1991–92 academic year, the learning support department was fortunate enough to take on 50 additional hours of LSA time. In the past, the in-class support had only been available in the lower school. With Louise, Susan and Linda moving into senior school and a number of other pupils with difficulties, it was vitally important that in-class support was available in the senior school.

Support structures

With seven GCSE options and no alternative curriculum provision, school life was going to be very difficult for the three pupils. Louise and Susan were the two pupils who above all were identified by all staff as not having the skills to cope with the demands of the formal curriculum. All three had very poor self-esteem. They viewed their lower school experience as a failure and could see little reason for working in the senior school.

In the first instance, Louise and Susan were the priorities regarding how to give them access to a very difficult curriculum. A high level of in-class support was set up for these two pupils. In a number of subjects, the support was carried out by myself as the only full-time teacher in the department. However, the two lessons of tutorial time and French were taught by the part-time teacher in the department. This teacher had also spent a large amount of time in the lower school with Louise and Susan. During French tutorial and some English lessons, the pupils were withdrawn from subject areas and taught in a group of two or three and on occasions individually.

An overview of the curriculum support for Susan and Louise

Both pupils are in the bottom maths group. This group has six lessons of maths. One of the doubles is taught by three maths specialists. There are 28 in the group. The other two doubles are taught by two maths specialists.

The science option is single. Against single science, two extra maths lessons are taught plus two tutorial lessons. The tutorial lessons are supervised by teaching staff. The staffing for tutorial times is generally the learning support co-ordinator and the senior teacher. These lessons give the pupils the opportunity to carry out coursework/homework with staff help. Time is also spent using the computer to facilitate keyboard skills and familiarise pupils with menu-driven software.

Support

- Maths: one double (three maths specialists), one double (two maths specialists plus LSA support), one double (two maths specialists plus LSA).
- English: Flexible arrangement. Withdrawn by teacher (LSC) or support in class to work in a small group.
- Science: Five lessons of support by teacher (LSC).
- Technology: Four lessons of support by a technology specialist.
- Geography: Two lessons of support (LSC). Three lessons LSA.
- French: Four lessons withdrawn taught in group of two by a teacher (one lesson LSA).

Art: Unsupported

At the beginning of Year 10, Louise had opted for PE. However, after a few lessons it became clear that this was going to be difficult. This was due to the academic demands of the theory, particularly anatomy and physiology, and the refusal of the pupil to participate in practicals. Negotiations took place to transfer her to art.

The first few lessons of art were very unsuccessful and it seemed that she might have to move out of the class. However, after reorganisation in the art department to accommodate their extremely high numbers and consider pupil needs in the most effective way, things settled down.

At this time the support of the outreach behaviour support teacher was particularly valuable. For two lessons a week, Louise was withdrawn from art and worked individually on her tasks with the help of the BST. This continued for two terms. It enabled the BST and the pupil to work together, and through the work to discuss Louise's behaviour in her other curriculum areas, to share ideas about strategies that were successful and unsuccessful, and to consider ways forward.

There was time for the BST to 'counsel' Louise. The interaction of the pupil and option at a specific point in time caused a problem.

Through intervention by the LSC and the BST, and the concern of the art department that Louise should managed to work in art, eventually without support, Louise successfully reintegrated for the full five lessons and worked independently until the end of the school year.

Success for Louise

Through the high level of support available, Louise has been enabled access to the curriculum. This has helped her learn about classroom conventions, stay on task and complete work. Her exercise books and files contain completed class and homework, encouraging her to continue working. She has the same amount of work as the motivated pupils have in their folders. She feels happy about her school work and manages to offer information orally in class without help. All this has raised her self-esteem.

Through maintaining homework in the tutorial time and in a flexible way during the French withdrawn lessons, for the first time in her school life Louise is not behind with school work. In test situations a reader scribe was used to enable information to be recorded. Similarly, information was put on to tape to help revision. This helped enormously and although in many subject areas results were still in the bottom end of the class, they were far better than any previous results. There was also a very good result by Louise in science.

Throughout the year, the concerns have moved to become satisfactory and in two areas praise. There are still one or two concerns, but the all-round improvement has been tremendous. When Louise is experiencing difficulty and behaviour has been inappropriate, the LSC has spent time discussing things with Louise. The head of year has also been very involved, encouraging positive behaviour, spending time discussing things with Louise. Whenever possible, praise has been used to reward effort and encourage further application.

Louise has always had a good attendance record and throughout this year this has been maintained. She had an internal suspension for one day and a short period on report after this, but this has been the only major occasion of poor behaviour. Many staff have commented on the overall improvement of Louise's classroom behaviour and improvement in her work. As a result of the huge increase in Louise's written work, her spelling and reading have also started to improve although she is still unable to work totally independently.

Susan improves

The support available for Susan has been much the same as Louise's. Susan has also benefited from two-and-a-half hours extra teacher time per week. This has been given as a result of her statement. In the same way as Louise has applied herself, so has Susan. However, Susan's improvement in self-esteem has also led to her requesting extra reading books and time for reading help. This has helped her reading enormously.

There has also been a dramatic difference in her attendance. She has had very little time away from school during the year. Her absences have been genuinely for illness.

Susan has also had one internal suspension. This was for two days and resulted from inappropriate behaviour towards other pupils. However, overall her general behaviour and application to work has once again improved.

Linda's progress

Towards the end of the autumn term of Year 10, many concerns had been raised about Linda. Her attendance was at a very low level. When she was in school she spent the majority of her time outside the classroom. She did not want to be at school and claimed to believe that her choice of future career would not be affected in any way by lack of qualifications. Linda had progressed to a functional level, although having a learning difficulty, and did not warrant the high level of support Louise and Susan had attracted. However, it was possible to extend support to her in science and maths and to withdraw her to work in the small group for English. She also had the help of the technology specialist in technology.

Through discussion and interest being shown in her, once again the reported incidents of poor behaviour were reduced. Her attendance again improved although by no means to 100 per cent. In conversation with the ESW, she reported, 'She liked to work in the small group and have help in class. She got her work done.' She also said, 'I'd like to do all my lessons in the study centre.' This is not possible and would not help her towards independence.

With all three pupils during the summer term when it was possible, work was organised so support could be withdrawn on occasions to enable the pupils to work and behave appropriately independently. Again this was generally successful. Linda had been working well with the support structure. Where it was not possible to support, because support was not in place and resources were limited, Linda experienced great difficulty in behaving appropriately and has had to be sent on a regular basis to the deputy head.

The Future for Louise, Susan and Linda

During the year, I have been investigating alternatives to GCSE for 14–16 year-olds with special educational needs. It has been very difficult to find something that can be used that will fit with National Curriculum criteria and given an accreditation.

Just after half term in the summer term, Louise, Susan and Linda as a group articulated their concerns regarding their curriculum, asking why they should continue to work hard as they would not be taking exams? Again concerns regarding some subject areas were raised with regard to their future employment. They knew they had tried hard, produced work and received acknowledgement for their work from staff. However, what was the point of doing this next year when they felt they would not be entered for GCSE?

Youth Award Scheme

This coincided with my investigations of the Youth Award Scheme (YAS). Discussions took place with senior management, particularly the senior teacher who has responsibility for curriculum planning and development.

We were considering trialling the award with these three pupils and perhaps a small number of Year 10 pupils. The bronze award is achievable using experiences such as work experience and setting subject-orientated work in line with a youth award challenge.

This way the pupils would also be following the National Curriculum but not taking a GCSE. The work could be achieved in option classes and in withdrawn groups. The two areas of the curriculum where the pupils felt they were not managing were social studies and French.

Staff in these areas also expressed their concerns, particularly for Linda as she did not have the support or appropriate behaviour. Year 11 was looking achievable regarding the setting up of the award.

The trial of the YAS

Going back to the pupils, I suggested they express their point of view regarding the curriculum to the senior teacher. They wrote him a letter and invited him to a meeting. It took a little while for the meeting to be set up as heads of departments and heads of year were given information about the award, the managing of timetable and what would be expected of option staff, in order that they could comment and express their opinions. There was overwhelming support for the trial of the YAS.

When staff support was evident, a meeting between the pupils and the senior teacher was arranged. The pupils explained how they felt and the senior teacher was able to offer them an alternative to the curriculum they had been following. He acknowledged that they had worked hard and explained they would have to continue to work hard but there would be more flexibility regarding the grouping and work carried out.

Through this work they could have help, and once their folders were finished the work could be submitted. They had every chance of achieving the Bronze Youth

Award. I feel that being able to offer this towards the end of Year 10 encouraged them to continue to work hard right up to the end of the year. With the YAS we are addressing their particular concerns and all being well will be able to accredit their success rather than reinforce failure through non-exam entry.

We have to hope that this will encourage the pupils to be motivated, to work throughout their Year 11 and avoid inappropriate behaviour. Realistically the support structure will need to remain in place to help them achieve this.

Note: Since September 1993, the Cooper School has been able to offer the Youth Award Scheme as alternatives to GCSE.

The Behaviour Support Teacher

The BST has a specific amount of time in the school each week, generally one morning and two afternoon sessions. This can be flexible, however, depending on the need of the pupils. Through referrals from year heads, deputies and myself, a timetable is negotiated to work with particular pupils. This could be on a long-term or a short-term basis. The work is varied and matches the activities noted by (Rennie 1992):

- withdrawing 'problem' children;
- counselling 'problem' children;
- supporting other staff in their classes;
- devising behaviour modification programmes;
- supporting individual children;
- advising other staff on class management.

This is the first year this type of support has been available in the school. A member of staff from an off-site unit is now working *in situ*. The off-site provision will remain but will be available for specific times of the week rather than full time. The emphasis is on working in mainstream.

After a few initial problems due to the rapid change in direction of the unit and limited preparation time, the work in school has been successful. Staff are referring more pupils as they see the benefits of the BST's support. Pupils who regularly cause concern have been able to manage their behaviour. There have also been instances when behaviourally difficult pupils have asked to see the BST themselves, as they know they will have support through a difficult patch.

A great deal of the work carried out by the BST takes place on a one-to-one basis. This will take place once a week for a period of time determined by the BST and the pupil. Discussions and meetings to review and plan this work take place weekly. The work carried out by the BST is available to any of the pupils within the school should it be necessary. All support undertaken by the BST needs the permission of the parent or guardian.

Through working on a Youth Award Challenge, the BST will have the opportunity to support the three pupils discussed above in their Year 11.

Gaining Access

This description of practice within the Cooper School has outlined one way of managing to enable EBD pupils to gain access to the curriculum. However, what we do need to recognise is that it is expensive for this to happen. Keeping EBD pupils in mainstream should not be seen as a cost-cutting exercise but as a positive development for the 'individuals'. This has to be properly resourced and services such as the BST maintained.

The reduction in statementing hours from the LEA has caused difficulties, with schools having to provide the first five hours. When pupils only receive five hours, the schools are maintaining these very difficult pupils almost totally. Schools need to be able to offer adequate staffing and commit themselves to the reality that some parts of the curriculum will need to be offered in groups as small as three or four.

Annual audits need to be carried out early on in the school year to identify the numbers of pupils requiring help and the type of help they need. If the figures are presented regularly and senior management staff and governors are aware of the resourcing necessary, they can begin to plan and implement suitable resourcing.

If the pupils are responding to the support structures, staff will support the extra financing for this type of work. Classes are more manageable, and teaching more effective when EBD pupils are involved in the curriculum and not causing distractions.

I do, however, believe that LEAs have a responsibility to these pupils, particularly statemented pupils. Withdrawing funds from these individuals could have a negative effect on staff in mainstream schools, encouraging them to ask why large amounts of money are spent on a few pupils. This could also encourage schools not to accept such pupils. This could result in EBD pupils being maintained in segregated provision rather than integrated in their local community school.

Acting as Advocates

To close, Roaf and Bines (1989) suggest that SEN staff in both mainstream and special schools should act as advocates for SEN pupils by arguing for the rights of children and young people with special needs. They believe staff should work to ensure that both policy and practice in schools reflect the implementation of those rights.

References

Ainscow, M (1990) 'Responding to Individual Needs', *British Journal of Special Education,* Vol 17, No 2.

Bines, H (1992) 'Developing roles in the new era', *Support for Learning,* Vol 7, No 2.

NCC Circular Number 5 (1989) *Implementing the National Curriculum - Participation by Pupils with Special Educational Needs,* NCC: York.

Rennie, E (1993) 'Behavioural Support Teaching: Points to Ponder', *Support for Learning,* Vol 8, No 1.

Roaf and Bines (1989) *Needs, Rights and Opportunities: Developing Approaches to Special Education,* Falmer Press: London.

ASDAN *YAS Youth Award Scheme,* Bristol University.

Further Reading

Dessent, T (1988) *Making the Ordinary School Special,* Falmer: East Sussex.

DES/NCC (1989) *A Curriculum for All.*

Gray, J and Richer, J (1988) *Classroom Responses to Disruptive Behaviour,* Macmillan: London.

Hanko, G (1987) *Special Needs in Ordinary Classrooms,* Basil Blackwell: Oxford.

Howard, P (1992) 'Challenging Behaviour Support', *Learning for All 2; Policies for Diversity in Education,* Eds Both, T, Swann, W, Masterton, M, and Potts, P (1992).

Mongon, D and Hart, S et al (1989) *Improving Classroom Behaviour: New Directions for Teachers and Pupils,* Cassell: London.

Thomas, G and Feiler, A *Planning for Special Needs: A Whole School Approach,* Basil Blackwell: Oxford.

PART TWO

ENSURING CURRICULUM ENTITLEMENT FOR PUPILS WITH EMOTIONAL AND BEHAVIOURAL DIFFICULTIES IN SPECIAL SCHOOLS

CHAPTER 4

Meeting the Curricular Needs of Pupils in a Special School (EBD) for Primary-Aged Children

By Roy Howarth

Northern House School

Northern House School educates and cares for boys and girls aged between 5 and 13 years. It was opened as a school for 'difficult children' in 1931 making it one of the oldest schools in England caring for children with emotional and behavioural difficulties. It moved to the present site in North Oxford in 1939, sharing the building with child guidance and other educational agencies.

It was not until 1983, following extensive renovation and rebuilding, that the site was used exclusively for the school. Since that time it has continued to expand. New classrooms have been added, allowing the roll to move up to 69 children. External services for reintegration and outreach now work with over 70 mainstream schools every year. The school runs inservice training days for primary school teachers and offers a wide range of training in primary, first, middle, secondary and upper schools.

Children are referred to Northern House because their emotional, behavioural and/or academic progress in their mainstream school has given cause for concern. At Northern House children make a fresh start in a small group situation which is supportive and protective. The environment is caring and consistent. Skilled specialist teachers encourage the children's development through carefully structured individual programmes of work. The resulting improvement in the children's self-image enables them to cope more effectively in their community.

The Fundamental Processes

In this chapter I shall describe the fundamental processes which I believe have been instrumental in helping to create the therapeutic environment described above. These processes, which have shaped the school we have today, are the same ones which have enabled us to tackle the extremely demanding task of introducing the National Curriculum.

At Northern House, the debate on the National Curriculum has focused on three questions:

* Given their difficulties, how appropriate is the National Curriculum for our pupils?
* How do we facilitate adequate access?
* What changes need to be made to school organisation to implement the National Curriculum?

In this chapter the debate which has taken place at Northern House over the past two years relating to the above questions will be described. The methods which we have used to reach a concensus over the best way to create an environment which enables our pupils to experience a wide curriculum will be explained. The topic model we initially designed for delivering the National Curriculum will be described, together with a brief analysis of one particular whole-school topic. The lessons learnt through an analysis of our initial model and the resulting new curriculum model will be discussed. The chapter will conclude with our hopes and fears for the future.

How Appropriate is the National Curriculum for Our Children?
The nature of EBD

Fundamental to any debate on the appropriateness of the National Curriculum to children with emotional and behavioural difficulties is an understanding of the nature of EBD. Mary Evans described it as follows. 'Within the heterogeneous group categorised as "maladjusted" (EBD) are pupils who are educationally retarded, academically brilliant, neurotic, delinquent, epileptic, psychotic, emotionally deprived and grossly over-indulged.' However, the majority of children display the following common difficulties:

* low self-esteem;
* poor academic self-image;
* poor concentration and academic under-attainment;

- poor interpersonal skills;
- lives which are often marked by conflict and/or deprivation at home and rejection at mainstream school.

It is therefore essential, if these children are to function effectively within their community, that the school attempts to counteract these emotional, academic and social deficits by:

- building for each child a positive self-image through academic and social success;
- creating an academic environment in which the child is successful;
- encouraging academic achievement and commitment to the learning process by offering a stimulating and extended curriculum;
- encouraging positive interpersonal experiences by building trusting staff/child relationships and organising co-operative group activities;
- communicating clearly and, wherever possible, positively with home.

The majority of children with EBD will work against the creation of the above as they have inbuilt and learnt behaviours which are contrary to normal responses. Their lack of success both socially and academically has built into their behaviour a lack of trust and confidence, both essential to the nurturing of healthy social and intellectual development.

Given the complexity of the problem and the need for our children to be given very careful, subtle and special treatment, would there not be a case for arguing that the National Curriculum would be so demanding that it would over-rule all our other work in the school?

The Debate

A curriculum meeting for teachers takes place every week. It lasts for just over an hour. The agendas are decided for the whole term. Much of the debate and planning surrounding the National Curriculum occurs in these meetings. The headteacher is almost always available for informal discussion.

Before the National Curriculum

Because of the nature of the problems they are dealing with, teachers of children with EBD have been tempted to adopt didactic teaching methods. Given the children's particular difficulties, they believed they were more settled when working either on individual programmes, involving little movement or interaction, or being taught clearly as a whole class. In the past at Northern House a considerable part of each day was spent on individual maths and English schemes. However, as the school grew in size, new teachers from mainstream primary schools were employed whose teaching philosophies were based more on a proactive, topic-based approach.

These new teachers questioned the didactic teaching style and narrow curriculum and argued, informally and in staff meetings, that if we were to effect real change in our pupils then we must spend more of the school day working on interactive skills, and encouraging the children to transfer skills. There was a feeling that a more challenging and varied curriculum might be instrumental in improving the child's motivation, and thus his or her self-image. Some staff believed that if the child's academic self-image improved, then improved behaviour would result. This debate had to be handled with sensitivity, as some teachers were being asked to look critically at their work. It was important to make them feel valued while encouraging them to take on board new ideas. Fortunately the casualties were few.

The more varied curriculum

It was agreed that we should introduce a more varied curriculum. Information technology, craft, design and technology, practical maths and science, music and drama gradually became regular features of the school day. Lessons were to last 35 minutes. A topic-based method of delivery was agreed to help with the transfer of skills and knowledge. More interactive teaching styles were encouraged across the whole curriculum.

More than half of the teachers went on the Oxfordshire Thinking Skills Programme and became convinced of the importance of developing the cognitive skills of our children. Staff who attended the training course reported back to the whole staff and emphasised the importance of encouraging children to think more about problem solving. They asked staff to consider the following questions:

- Do I give children a good range of opportunities to think and solve problems?
- Do I encourage them to plan their work?
- Do I ask them to evaluate methods and evidence?
- Do I ensure they apply skills and knowledge they have acquired elsewhere?
- Do I give children the opportunity to communicate their ideas, experiences and feelings in a variety of ways?
- Do I encourage them to listen to each other?
- Do I give them opportunities to co-operate with each other and other people?
- Do I ask them to make judgements and reflect critically on what they have achieved?
- Do I encourage individuals to support one another?

Evaluation

An evaluation of the changes made in the curriculum and our methods of delivering it, held at an extended staff meeting lasting three hours (with wine and sticky cakes at the end as a reward), elicited both negative and positive feedback.

Positives
- Children being more interested, motivated, and able to cope with interactive situations.
- Teachers finding the day more varied, challenging and stimulating.
- The demands of the wider curriculum generating a recognition of the need to resource our teaching by forward planning.

Concerns
- Teachers concerned about planning, differentiation, record keeping and continuity between groups.
- Children, used to individual work and didactic teaching styles, with poor social skills and poor self-control, giving staff headaches in more practical sessions.

It was at this point that we were faced with the task of considering introducing the National Curriculum into the school.

Fundamental factors in our debate on the relevance of the National Curriculum to our children

We had reached a point in the development of our school's curriculum where we were searching for a clear structure. Would the National Curriculum offer us that structure?

- We aim to return at least 50 per cent of our pupils to mainstream education, so it is essential for them to be fully participating in the same educational process.
- We are a day school, so out of school children mix with their local neighbourhood friends. They have to cope with 'you go to a special school' taunts. To be able to share similar experiences of school work greatly enhances their self-image.
- We run an active pre-integration programme where 20 per cent of our children attend mainstream school to participate in one or two lessons a week. During their visits the children must actively take part in the lesson they attend. Experience of and familiarity with National Curriculum topics greatly enhances their self-confidence.

63

- The school is seen as a place where children 'get better'. To separate them from the mainstream by disapplying the National Curriculum would be setting them apart.
- The majority of our children come from backgrounds which are intellectually impoverished. The wider, more challenging and more focused the curriculum, the better.

There is a clear recognition from all staff that Northern House is *a school,* and that the most effective therapy we, as teachers, can offer our troubled children is to make them feel academically successful and 'good' at school. The experience of the staff has reinforced the belief that if children are successful at 'their work', believe they are progressing academically and feel that they are doing similar work to their friends and relations in mainstream, then they begin to 'get better'.

The staff feel that the National Curriculum presents them with a valid and easily read structure from which to create stimulating programmes of study. The progressive nature of the structure allows long-term planning and facilitates thorough and consistent recording of individual and group development. If correctly co-ordinated and taught in a way which caters for the special needs of our pupils, we believe that:

The National Curriculum must take a prime place in a special school for EBD children because it acts as a symbol of the normal process of education. It gives to the pupil and the teacher a sense of a proper educational environment. It is a therapeutic tool which can give the environment of the special school authenticity. It has a commonality with all other schools which bridges the gap between special and mainstream education.

How Do We Facilitate Access to the National Curriculum?

I described above how, through the system of debate at our weekly staff meetings, encouraged by the input of young mainstream teaching staff and our experience of the Oxfordshire Thinking Skills Programme, we had been steadily moving towards the decision to offer our children as broad a curriculum as any good mainstream school, in a way which encourages:

- the acquisition of knowledge and skills and concepts;
- learning through firsthand experience;
- development of critical and creative thinking;
- linking new knowledge with existing knowledge;
- development of interpersonal skills.

The responsibility of delivering the National Curriculum clearly presented us with an immediate, unavoidable and challenging number of problems. Given the problems our children display and their fundamental need for an environment which is safe and predictable, satisfactorily delivering a curriculum as varied, complex and challenging as the National Curriculum without first establishing very clearly the parameters of behaviour and work expectations for staff and children, would be an impossible task.

Unhappy, confused, distracted, disorganised, unmotivated children do not learn. The ethos of the school must be easily read by both teachers and pupils and the process partially owned by them for it to be an effective therapeutic environment.

Creating a Safe and Consistent Framework in Which Children Can Learn

The ethos of Northern House School is to create a caring and consistent environment in which children can come to terms with and overcome their difficulties. Consistency is felt to be a key factor in helping the children to feel safe. We adopted several strategies for attaining this consistency.

The staff handbook

It was thought appropriate by all the staff to negotiate agreed working practices. Five staff meetings, chaired by myself, were designated for this work. At these meetings the content of the staff handbook was rigorously debated. Debate was honest, open and sometimes heated. The main areas to be covered were identified by the staff, and working parties were set up to write sections for the handbook. These submissions were then discussed by the whole staff. Nothing went into the handbook until it had been agreed by all the staff as good work practice. The introduction of the staff handbook reads as follows:

This handbook, created and written by the whole staff, is intended to guide staff in relation to working practice in the school. To be supportive, informative, bringing to the school a uniformity of action and response in relation to children. It is hoped it will act as a creative aid to the development of a therapeutic environment in which children are able to grow and change.

The handbook written by the staff, for the staff, describes in detail not only the academic environment but also social expectations, the desired conduct of adults/children and the processes staff are expected to follow. The 22-page document is reviewed annually and reprinted in a different format each year.

One of the tasks staff undertook while debating the handbook was to list the school's general expectations of staff. The resulting list follows.

The school's expectation of the staff:

- *participation in school policy making*
- *participation in school curriculum development*
- *participation in staff development*
- *supervision of children has priority over staff breaks*
- *covering for breaks*
- *case conferences/external meetings outside school hours*
- *supporting children in mainstream school*
- *taking children home during school hours or after school*
- *mutual support and trust of all staff*
- *creating a warm, caring, positive environment for the children.*

All staff should be good time-keepers. For other duties see Health and Safety Report.

The children's handbook

A similar handbook has also been written by children, for children, which again describes the environment in which learning takes place. The older children in the school take part in a discussion assembly with their teachers and myself each week. Several such assemblies were spent on agreeing the content of the handbook. The contents were then given to all the classes in the school to rewrite, decorate and add sections to. This was written by children as to a new child advising him or her of the school's expectations, both academic and social. The example below expresses to new children and parents how the children view the school.

1. *My School*
   I work in a special school which cares for children who have difficulties managing in a mainstream school. My school helps me to overcome the problems I have had in the past.

Northern House helps me to:

1. *Understand all about my behaviour.*
2. *Experience new areas of interest.*
3. *Improve my school work by giving me time to develop my skills.*
4. *Understand the needs of other people including parents, teachers and other children.*

> *The aim of Northern House School is to help me grow into a more successful person.*

The staff and pupil handbooks describe how each group sees its responsibilities to the school, and clarifies in writing the processes which are followed. They are a reference point on agreed practices and can be referred to at any time. There are a number of other systems which are used to make the environment more objective and consistent for adults and children.

Positive reinforcement
Points sheets

This is a system of assessing each child three times a day on their social skills and attitude to work. I was introduced to a similar system during a professional visit to the United States of America. I presented the system to the staff and they felt that it would be interesting to give it a try. The results were positive so the system was adopted, though we modified the criteria to suit our population. Long discussions took place with children and staff to identify the values specific to the school.

The following expectations were agreed:

* doing as asked straight away;
* being sociable and friendly;
* setting a good example;
* ignoring silliness;
* moving around sensibly.

If a child achieves the stated number of points then he or she is awarded at the end of that week with a gold smiling face sticker. These are displayed on a gold smiley face card which always has the theme of the term's National Curriculum topic as a background. If a child achieves a stated number of gold faces in a half term, he or she will be taken on a Smiling Face treat. This can be anything from ice-skating to pond-dipping to climbing White Horse Hill.

Trophies

At the end of every week a Smiling Face trophy is awarded to the child with the most behaviour points. This is given in the Friday Reward Assembly. Also the Diamond Award trophy is given to the child who has made the most effort with behaviour in the week (with the emphasis being on effort and progress). These children are given a special letter to take home.

Credit system

This was negotiated with and is used by the staff as a marking system for all forms of academic performance from PE to maths. Children are given an 'A' for good work. These A's are recorded in a book and certificates are given in the Friday Reward Assembly for 25, 50, 100, 150 up to 400 credits. The certificates are valued greatly by the children. The criteria for achieving an A were agreed with the pupils at their discussion assemblies with the head or deputy:

- start work straight away;
- be attentive and listen;
- work hard and concentrate;
- work neatly;
- co-operate in group work;
- be able to work on your own.

Once a term the positive reinforcement systems are reviewed in a staff meeting. Criteria may be changed, and inconsistencies in awarding credits are aired openly.

Incident sheets

These are completed every time a child disturbs a lesson. They are based on the antecedents–behaviour–consequence model. Behaviour is weighted on a scale from one to four as follows:

Weighting One
- Consistent abuse anywhere in the school
- Swearing anywhere in the school
- Mild physical assault on a child
- Ongoing disruption in or out of class
- Behavioural requiring the removal of a child for a short period of time
- Failure to match behaviour targets set on weekly sheets

Weighting Two
- Behaviour requiring the child to be removed from the classroom or any other part of the school, serious enough to need time out with the attendance of an adult

Weighting Three
- Temper tantrum requiring the management of more than one adult
- Running away but only within the confines of the school boundary fence

---

Weighting Four
- Running away beyond the boundary fence of the school
- Climbing on an adjoining building
- Deliberate assault on a member of staff whether in a temper tantrum or not

Each sheet is signed by the adult involved with the behaviour and countersigned by the class teacher. With some persistently troublesome children we focus on specifically identified minor behaviours, all at weighting of one. These are described on a Type A incident sheet. All sheets are read and signed by me. Each child's incident profile is produced each half term and records are kept of the pattern of incidents.

Behaviour scores
These are completed once a term jointly by the teacher and his or her classroom assistant. They assess levels of functioning in three main areas: emotional, learning and conduct.

Groups
The school has eight classes of between six and nine children, each managed by a teacher and a classroom assistant. Groups are created using many different criteria:

1. age;
2. academic ability;
3. teacher's skills and preference;
4. mix of children;
5. severity of condition.

Time and care are taken in the selection of groups. Senior members of staff compile the initial class lists which are then circulated to all staff. Staff then have a period of several days in which to talk to the head about concerns. The groups are often modified on the basis of these discussions. No one criteria predominates but a workable solution is normally achieved. As we admit up to 25 children each year, it is necessary to periodically make minor adjustments to groups, in order to accommodate these new children, but we aim to maintain a stable core in each group during the academic year.

The systems described above have been set up at Northern House to help our children to feel secure enough to access the National Curriculum. It is our experience that by having

- high expectations;
- clear expectations;

- a positive reward system;
- whole school expectations;

and by making every pupil feel valued and important, even very difficult children can positively experience the wider curriculum.

The Teacher's Skills

The second essential factor in the successful delivery of a wide curriculum to children with EBD is the skill of the teacher. Learning can only take place in a quiet and controlled environment. This is partly achieved by fair, caring and consistent school expectations, but the skill of the individual teacher is of paramount importance.

During our weekly staff meetings issues of control of individual children and of specific groups are regularly discussed. Children with EBD constantly test a teacher's competence and confidence. It is essential if we are to effect real change in our pupils, and remain sane as teachers, that we have very high expectations of ourselves. As a staff we agreed on the importance of the following skills:

- high academic and behavioural expectations;
- frequent recognition of effort and success;
- good organisation and management within the classroom;
- ability to pre-empt trouble by constant scanning;
- a calm, pleasant manner;
- a sense of humour and the ability to diffuse rather than escalate;
- ability to carefully tailor work to children's individual needs to ensure success;
- an ability to be fair and consistent.

These skills are not always naturally part of the repertoire of teachers who are appointed to Northern House, therefore a programme of staff meetings and inservice training is carefully designed to enable new staff to understand the school's ethos and methods of working.

INSET

During the last year INSET days or INSET evenings have included our school doctor talking about child abuse, National Curriculum advisers discussing planning and delivery of the curriculum, debates on our behaviour management systems, and several long sessions on assessing and recording National Curriculum levels.

Team teaching

The most effective way of passing on these subtle skills to new staff is by ensuring that new teachers team-teach for at least their first term with an experienced and highly skilled teacher. This enables the new teacher to assimilate and practice complex skills and learn the complexities of the structures operating within the school, before having to take on the additional load of sole responsibility for the discipline and management of a group.

As a consequence of the structures described above, a readable, fair and predictable environment is created. This enables new children admitted to the school, often with quite complex and violent disorders, to settle very quickly. Often the referring symptoms lessen and the child feels secure. It is not unknown for some children never to produce the referring symptom within the environment of Northern House.

What Changes Need to Be Made to the School Organisation to Implement the National Curriculum?

We agree within the school that if the planning and delivery of the curriculum are right then everything else will fall into place. If the process of learning is adequately structured, co-ordinated, clear, intellectually challenging at the correct level for the individual child, and most of all developed and owned by the teachers, then teaching becomes a more pleasurable and predictable activity.

Our planning approach to the National Curriculum

The fundamental change has been the amount of staff time spent on planning the curriculum. Because the average length of stay at Northern House is three years, it was thought appropriate to manage the curriculum over that period of time. This would give the child a chance to experience a wide curriculum with no repeats. It was important that staff approved the content of the cycle and felt supported by an effective curriculum team.

It was decided to use the science curriculum as the source of the topic titles, thus ensuring that the science curriculum was adequately covered. From that core all cross-curricular networks could be designed. The topics selected were:

Communication and the senses   Ourselves
Variety of life (1) Plants   Magnetism/electricity
Materials   Variety of life (2) Animals
Movement and forces   Earth and atmosphere
Environment and pollution

Making a network

At the beginning of each term we used half of our INSET day to build a network based on the identified topic for the following term. Workshops tackled different areas and then reported back to the whole staff. This network was then discussed in more detail at the Tuesday curriculum meetings.

The Tuesday planning meetings

The subject specialist's role

The weekly curriculum staff meeting became a crucial part of the school week, for it was at these meetings that all curriculum preparation was undertaken. The sharing and the developing of ideas produced in the staff a feeling of ownership of content and direction. Some of the meetings were for whole staff, others were for subject specialists.

From the beginning it was agreed to work at least one term in advance. For example, all preparation for the spring term was completed by the end of the summer term. Subject specialists produced broad schemes of work for the whole school. This preparation included the ordering of all materials, the booking of visits wherever possible and the recording of the appropriate television programmes. It meant the acquiring of all source material well in advance of use. The most powerful effect of this was to relieve the pressure of preparation.

The class teacher's role

Curriculum specialists distribute detailed networks to class teachers. Each teacher then produces, from the network, a sequence matrix for their own group's work for the term. This is made available to the whole staff for cross-reference, time-tabling, use of resources and collaboration.

The Victorian Topic
An example of a class teacher's matrix for the second half of term
CLASS B - AUTUMN TERM (SHEET 2)

Weeks	Maths	English	RE	History	Science	Technology	Art	Geography	Music	Drama
6	Estimation and checking of standard imperial measures	Posters: Make a poster advertising a firework display	Buddhism: festivals and ceremonies	Schooling in Victorian times	Clay (2): Testing physical properties, moulding and joining clay	Yarn wrapping (2)	Designing a Victorian table decoration (1)	Metals	Firework music: Listen and create	Firework drama: Music and movement
7	Comparison of standard and non-standard measures	Notes: Write a note explaining absence from school	Hinduism: festivals and ceremonies (1)	Victorian families	Metals (1): Sorting and testing physical properties of various metals	Victorian recipe	Designing a Victorian table decoration (2)	Oil	Victorian playground rhymes	The Victorian family
8	Measuring continued	Lists: Write a list of presents you would like to buy for family and friends	Hinduism: festivals and ceremonies (2)	City children and middle class children	Fabrics (1): Sorting and testing different fabrics	Victorian recipe (2)	Objective drawing of a Victorian artefact	Oil	Work for assembly	Work for assembly
9	Use of child's own standard measures	Lists: Make a list of ingredients needed for our Victorian recipe	Judaism: festivals and ceremonies (1)	Entertainment and pastimes	Fabrics (2): Sorting and testing different fabrics	Bread: dough garland (1)	Making Victorian wallpaper	Water	Christmas play: Victorian	Christmas play
10	Choosing appropriate standard measures	Letters: Write a letter to a friend	Judaism: festivals and ceremonies (2)	Victorian toys	Choosing correct materials (1): Testing materials for electrical conductivity	Bread: dough garland (2)	Drawing portraits in a Victorian style	Water	Christmas play	Christmas play
11	Comparison and conversion of standard measures	Letters: Write a letter inviting people to the Christmas play	Christmas: preparations and activities (1)	Victorian Christmas	Choosing correct materials (2): Testing materials for conduction of heat	Christmas preparations and activities	Making Christmas cards (1)	Test	Christmas play	Christmas play
12	Comparison and conversion of standard measures	Letters: Write a letter to Father Christmas	Christmas: preparations and activities (2)	Victorian Christmas		Christmas preparations and activities	Making Christmas cards (2)	Test	Nativity	Nativity

The matrix shows one teacher's planning. As our children find it difficult to recall and transfer information, we aim for as many cross-curricular links as possible. We also teach in subject areas. Our children cope best with short, very focused lessons and respond to the differing challenges of the different disciplines.

Evaluation: Did the Victorian topic work?

Positives
- Because of our forward planning we had a good set of bright and stimulating text books, and a collection of artefacts from the museum resource. Staff used these to generate discussion and then gave differentiated worksheets for follow-up.
- The topic lent itself to stimulating visits. Not the easiest undertaking given the children's EBD, but an excellent way of generating interest. The children enjoyed the visits to Stoke Bruerne canal museum and the day in the Victorian classroom. They also particularly enjoyed handling Victorian artefacts, including a Victorian musical box, and looking at our own schoolhouse which dates from Victorian times.
- In drama children pretended to be living on working barges, and experienced the difficulties of living in such a confined space. They also worked as chimney sweeps, crawling through confined spaces and frequently getting stuck.
- The tie-in with the Christmas play ('Scrooge') and decorating Northern House in the Victorian manner gave the topic considerable life and reinforced the whole-school ethos.
- Staff felt that the cross-curricular links with English, CDT, drama and music were satisfactory, and that the children's understanding of the topic was enhanced by the resulting repetition and reinforcement.

Concerns
- Science and geography had not linked in at all. This was because we were over two-thirds of the way through our three-year cycle and the need to cover certain topics was superceding our plan to deliver the curriculum in a cross-curricular way.
- There was a feeling that the topic had not covered enough National Curriculum Attainment Targets (ATs).
- There was a growing feeling that the three-year cycle based on science topics was too contrived.

Delivering the National Curriculum: Our Current Position
The four-year plan

Whole-staff evaluation after the completion of the three-year cycle raised the following points:

- Staff felt that we were trying to cover too much ground in the three-year cycle, that ATs were being skated over and that a four-year cycle would be better.
- It was agreed, after a long and heated discussion, that always using a science attainment target as the central focus for each terms' topic meant that the cross-curricular links were sometimes (to say the least) tenuous, and that other curriculum areas carried less weight. Staff felt that genuine cross-curricular links were of fundamental importance when designing a topic. They believed that for our children, with their problems of poor academic self-image, poor concentration, difficulty with retaining information and difficulty with transferring knowledge, it was essential that cross-curricular links were genuine, not contrived.
- Staff decided to look at the National Curriculum from a different angle. They decided to identify broad cross-curricular topics which they felt would appeal to the children and then make a web, linking in National Curriculum ATs. They did an experimental draft of a four-year topic cycle and discovered that it was possible to effectively cover the majority of ATs by this process.

The following topics were chosen by the whole staff as being appealing to both teachers and children and workable.

Spring 94	Exploration and encounters
Summer 94	Space, earth and atmosphere
Autumn 94	Invaders and settlers (Romans)
Spring 95	Food and farming (Vikings)
Summer 95	Water
Autumn 95	Celebrations
Spring 96	Our environment
Summer 96	Olympics
Autumn 96	Houses and homes
Spring 97	Egyptians
Summer 97	Underground/overground
Autumn 97	Ourselves in the community

As a planning exercise and to see whether the majority of ATs would be covered by these topics, the Tuesday curriculum group made topic webs and identified ATs relevant to the topic. The following is an example of one such web.

A Summary of the Network for Summer 1996: Olympics

Science	Technology	Geography	History	English	Maths	PE	Art
Forces	Olympic medals	Continents	Ancient Greece	Greek myths	Handling data	Mini-Olympics	Posters to advertise Olympus
Gravity	National dress for opening ceremony	Countries	Olympic Games	Similarities/ difference Olympics	Recording	Fantasy countries	Tag for trainers
Natural, man-made forces	Design a torch for the Olympic flame	Oceans and seas	Greece — home of Olympics		Presenting results	(RE) IBM ten-step award 8-10 years	Greek gods
Pushes, pulls	Cheerleaders	Routes to Olympic City	Greeks at sea		Present statistics to follow Olympic golds etc		Masks
Stop, start, speed	Olympic flag		Democracy, The Parthenon, cities		Different events		Toy mascot for Olympics
Road Safety	T-shirt for mini-Olympics		Markets and shops		Volume/mass		Sports paintings
Movement of the body, body facts, and muscles and joints			War with Persia				Signs for Olympic City
Fiction: Archimedes			Warships, Sparta, Battle of Salanus				Rosettes for mini-Olympics
Column/mass of objects on water			Everyday life in Ancient Greece				
			Greeks at work				
			Greek houses				
			Greek gods				
				VISIT British Museum, Ashmolean	TV Zig Zag Summer '91	Greeks	

This exercise reinforced the belief that a four-year plan would ensure a much more adequate covering of the curriculum than a three-year cycle.

Detailed planning

Staff felt happy with the planning system which had evolved during the three-year curriculum trial. This included topic webs, cross-curricular grids for classes and termly evaluation.

Tuesday meetings

Now that the topic webs have been designed for the next four years, it has been decided to use the Tuesday meetings to expand the following term's web, develop materials, order books, collect artefacts, foresee and solve any problems. Evaluation is to be ongoing.

The staff have also decided to look at the school's curriculum philosophy. Each subject specialist will give a detailed description of their area of the curriculum. It is felt that this exercise, as well as being helpful to new staff, will enable teachers to improve their knowledge of the whole curriculum.

Resourcing

Now that the four-year topic plan is complete, the school is able to plan resources more efficiently and fairly. This will enable subject areas to be adequately resourced so that staff have the appropriate books and equipment for delivering the curriculum in a stimulating way.

Differentiation

During our discussions strong concerns about differentiation were voiced. We agreed that it is the class teacher's (or in some areas subject specialist's) responsibility to differentiate the work. This is relatively easy in maths and English where there are differentiated work and text books. In other subject areas, teachers tend to make worksheets at varying levels of difficulty, use the learning support assistant to take groups, have differing expectations for different children, and encourage some children to work more independently. As a school we are critical of the quality of our differentiation and recognise a need to work on this area.

Record keeping

All the legal demands of the education acts are accommodated in the school's system of record keeping. This involves the upkeep of two major documents.

Pupil profiles

These have been designed specifically for the pupils and give details and evidence of National Curriculum Attainment Targets achieved. These are updated every half term. They were designed and produced by our curriculum leader and a new teacher who had worked with the National Curriculum in mainstream. The initial design was presented to and discussed by the whole staff before being produced in bulk.

Class record books

These contain a description in detail of all attainment targets achieved within the group. They are used as working documents and are used on a daily basis. They enable a class teacher to have an instant view of the levels of attainment, and areas covered in each subject, making it easier to organise differentiated teaching, as the example for English shows:

English

NAMES

LEVELS		ATTAINMENT TARGET 2 READING									
1	a	Recognise that print is used to carry meaning, in books and in other forms in the everyday world.									
	b	Begin to recognise individual words or letters in familiar contexts.									
	c	Show signs of a developing interest in reading.									
	d	Talk in simple terms about the content of stories, or information in non-fiction books.									
2	a	Read accurately and understand straightforward signs, labels and notices.									
	b	Demonstrate knowledge of the alphabet in using word books and simple dictionaries.									
	c	Use picture and context cues, words recognised on sight and phonic cues in reading.									
	d	Describe what has happened in a story and predict what may happen next.									
	e	Listen and respond to stories, poems and other material read aloud, expressing opinions informed by what has been read.									
	f	Read a range of material with some independence, fluency, accuracy and understanding.									

Continuous assessment

We also practice continuous assessment through schemes of work such as Ginn English and maths, and we annually assess children on nationally standardised tests.

Informing parents

We use various methods of communication with parents to keep informed of their child's progress:

- the annual review procedure of the 1981 Education Act;
- annual school reports sent home stating National Curriculum levels of achievement;
- parent evenings;
- daytime parents interviews;
- homework, keeping parents in touch with their child's academic levels;
- pupil profiles along with results from standardised test always available in school;
- home-school diaries plus regular phone calls.

Assessment of Success of Adapting to the National Curriculum

Teacher attitude and working practice

Teachers feel very positive about the National Curriculum — even teachers who were initially cynical. They report their groups are easier to manage, better motivated, and more on task. They themselves feel challenged and stimulated by the wider curriculum, and the task of delivering it in a way which is appropriate for their group.

Administrative structure now attached to academic process

The demands of the National Curriculum in terms of clear planning and recording have necessitated the setting up of a clear and detailed administrative process. Although this is demanding of time and effort, staff feel they have clear direction and are able to be accountable with confidence.

Academic improvements in performance attitude and self-image

Over half the children in the school spend some time in mainstream. They functionally integrate, and are at ease with a familiar curriculum. Fourteen children are at present on pre-integration programmes and 18 have started integrating into their local mainstream schools. At Northern House, children are generally interested and well-motivated, and the number of incidents of difficult behaviour has decreased.

Conclusion

Northern House School educates children who have failed in mainstream school. They arrive with low confidence, are anxious and have under-attained academically. They have difficulties relating to adults and children.

Given this population, it might seem ambitious to try to emulate a good mainstream primary school. Should we not develop a completely different way of helping these troubled children? Is a normal mainstream curriculum appropriate to pupils with EBD?

The school aims to help its pupils to become better adjusted so that they can fit more easily into their local community. Many of them return to their local mainstream school. It is essential for them to have access to the same curriculum as any other child. The concession we must make to the problems of our children is to ensure that we present the curriculum in a way which ensures success and consequently the development of a positive self-image.

We are blessed at Northern House with high staff/pupil ratio, and a highly skilled and committed staff. This alone would not ensure the successful delivery of the wide curriculum. However, over the past two years we have worked hard to try to improve our performance in this area. By encouraging supportive adult/adult, adult/child relationships, by establishing agreed standards and working practices, by careful planning and by having high expectations, we have moved some distance towards enabling all our children to experience a degree of academic success.

CHAPTER 5

Meeting the Curricular Needs of Pupils in a Residential Special School for Secondary-Aged Pupils

By Mike Samuels

Enborne Lodge

In this chapter I will describe a maintained boarding school for bright secondary-aged boys with emotional and behavioural difficulties and relate the effects of the National Curriculum on our pupils and discuss whether it meets their special needs.

For teachers who refer pupils to residential EBD schools, there is often an idea that such establishments represent a last resort for children who cannot be maintained in mainstream or whose problems are so intractable that they adversely affect the learning of their peers in ordinary school communities. Schools like Enborne Lodge are often seen as a last resort for 'the untreatable'.

We do not subscribe to this view. Those of us in the work, while not wanting to retain a medical model of our pupils' problems, nonetheless feel that it is meaningful to talk about special boarding schools as effecting a 'cure' for our pupils. We believe we use education in its broadest sense to bring about permanent change in the boys we work with and that we can 'teach' them to deal with their emotions and their difficulties.

We use as a starting point RS Peters' (1966) conceptual analysis of teaching as involving at least three components: a) to bring about knowledge and understanding b) by rational means c) taking into account the state of the learner. It is, of course, the problems of the learner and his learning strategies that we engage with.

The Pupils

The children we admit to Enborne Lodge display a wide range of antisocial behaviour patterns and problems of character and temperament. Nowadays they are sent to us with a description of their needs but to the general public, people closely associated with them and the teachers who in their previous schools have been driven to distraction by them, their presentation of symptoms is all too clear. They often lie, steal and cheat, they have temper tantrums, are destructive and are often cruel to each other. If they are not aggressive, quarrelsome and vindictive they can be shy, withdrawn, phobic or manipulative.

Statementing

They come to us nowadays as the tiny proportion of 'statemented' children for whom it is deemed that access to the National Curriculum is only possible if they learn and live away from home during term time. The processes by which statements are drawn up follow the procedures outlined by the 1981 Education Act. This date marks a watershed in the perceptions of these children as having needs which should be met rather than as having a disability which must be catered for. Prior to 1981 children were 'ascertained' and professionals decided what was best for them.

The process of drawing up a statement which involves multi-disciplinary assessments shares the onus of meeting the child's needs more equally with the child and the family. While this process is more in accordance with children's rights, it often places a heavy burden of responsibility and guilt on parents who have to agree, in the case of our pupils, to be seen to be acquiescing in a decision to send a child away from home.

The writing of a statement is often the culmination of many years of previous attempts to help a child and the initiative for a draft statement most often comes from the professionals, psychologists and teachers who work in the schools. It is no surprise that this is the case, because it is in the social milieu of a school and the necessary interaction of the child with the learning process, his or her peer group and other adults that the problems are seen to be most acute.

Families seeking help

Occasionally families seek help first for themselves in Child Guidance Clinics or go into family therapy, but as opportunities to avail themselves of this kind of help in the community diminish, this is nowadays less often the case. Alternatively, our pupils may first draw attention to themselves in social services departments or the courts if the way they signal their discomfiture attracts the attention of society at large.

The power of the problems

Whatever their routes to the residential school for EBD, there are some universals which seem to apply and are borne out by the statements. The power of the children's problems is often attested to by their previous schools' contribution to the full assessment. The children are typically described as 'hostile to teachers', 'undermining all attempts to help them', 'disruptive to the learning process of their peers'. Many of these descriptions are akin to the faulty learning strategies described by Denis Stott (1978).

Reading these statements, it is often hard to determine whether the emotional needs of the child impinge more heavily on their teachers than their presentation of conduct and learning disorders. One universal that does emerge is that the children nearly always have learning difficulties, sometimes perceived as being a contributory cause of their problems and sometimes seen as a consequence of them.

Family history

The families of emotionally disturbed children, unlike those of children with physical handicaps, do not have a great deal of sympathy extended to them, being seen as blameworthy rather than as victims. To some extent this is understandable. For a large proportion of the children that we deal with, the causes of their difficulties are clearly rooted in the dynamics of their early histories and their families.

This is, however, not always so. There are some families who have reared siblings of the child successfully and where there are no clear indications that they have contributed to the aetiology of the child's problems. A large proportion of the families, though, do have what are regarded as 'risk' factors and an admixture of variables which contribute to their children's difficulties. Many are single parents; many have marital problems or financial difficulties; many have a history of poor parenting themselves. Some have adopted children whose early damage becomes apparent later. Some are over-indulgent; some are over-punitive. They may be inconsistent, delinquent, depressed or physically frail.

The Staff

Enborne Lodge refers to itself as 'a community', as this is the best way we can manage to convey the sense that, although we have statutory responsibilities as a school, we are also aware that our pupils, who are with us on a 24-hour and seven-days-a-week basis during term time, are in some sense, because of the nature of their problems, reworking some of the experiences they would have had in a family.

On the other hand, families exist for the well-being of all members, adults and children alike. Our school exists solely for the children.

A multi-disciplinary team

We are staffed by a multi-disciplinary team which provides a 24-hour curriculum — much wider, of course, than anything envisaged by the confines of the National Curriculum. Adults in the community, to some degree, are all involved as role models for the pupils but also act as surrogate parents who nonetheless can retain a degree of objectivity about the children in their care. The team comprises teachers, child care staff and others who directly provide for the children's well-being and primary needs for food, clothes and medical attention. In addition, manual workers and administrators figure largely in such establishments and often present as adults with skills to whom the children can relate.

Personal qualities of staff

The curriculum is delivered in a much broader sense, therefore, than in ordinary schools and in theory is part of the children's programme from the minute they open their eyes in the morning until they go to bed at night — and sometimes into the small hours.

The National Curriculum prescribes what children should be taught, not how they should be taught. There are particular qualities which staff in special boarding schools have which are perhaps more important than the content of what they impart to the children.

In a study of a large number of special schools, Mary Wilson and Mary Evans observed in a Schools' Council Working Paper (No 65, 1980) 'that successful practitioners working with disturbed children showed an ability to endure in work which was very demanding. They appear to have a reserve of emotional strength and resilience which enabled them to mobilise warm feelings of concern for children in difficulty' and 'were not easily drawn into the collusive and manipulative mechanisms exhibited by the children.'

We can identify qualities such as caring, calmness, a sense of humour and honesty as vital characteristics of successful staff and, almost without exception, those staff who are prepared to listen attentively to what our pupils say are the ones who are most trusted by the boys. I suspect that many of the strengths of good staff in this establishment are the same as those elsewhere. We benefit, however, from a teacher/pupil ratio of 1:6 with additional teachers for curricular protection and with a parallel staff of up to ten child care workers for out-of-class activities. This enables us in a boarding school to provide a total milieu for a child which is inconceivable in a day special school where the child's problems are revivified daily at school and at home.

Teaching staff structure

In a special school, the teachers and their teaching style have to be special as well. A typically community for 40 boys is normally staffed to DfE standards by 6.7 full-time equivalent teachers. In our school, prior to the advent of the National Curriculum, we were able to offer a menu of around a dozen examinable subjects in addition to some areas which are not formally examined, such as sport, music and drama. Prior to 1985 the intake was mixed-ability, with as many boys in the 'superior' intelligence range as those who needed a large remedial input.

From this it can be seen that our teaching staff structure necessitated the appointment of teachers who had more than one specialism and also teachers who could take their subject to public examination level.

Nowhere in the training of teachers nationally is there an expectation that someone could teach to this level, for example, English, maths, rural science and drama. Yet such a teacher was appointed. The difficulty of juggling these curricular needs is enormous and when a member of staff left or gained promotion, we had to plug a large gap.

As if these demands were not great enough in themselves we also required teachers who could cope successfully or were qualified to deal with the emotional needs of our pupils as well as to work an extended teaching day.

More recently, we have had some enhancement from our local education authority to our teaching allocation and we now take in brighter pupils, but to cover the curriculum also requires the appointment of more part-time staff. This has led to a much richer diet for our pupils, but there are dangers in appointing too many part-time staff partly because staff appointed specifically to fulfil curricular obligations do not usually have SEN training and, more importantly, do not have the continuity of contact that our pupils need on a daily basis.

What makes a success?

There remain some intangible qualities that mark out successful teachers in our school. Many years ago, when we first opened a new teaching area, the first post holder was pressed upon us by the inspector as being 'as good a teacher as we are likely to find', having had full special educational needs training and successful

85

experience with deprived youngsters in a range of institutions. The teacher was given a merciful release within half a term! He was replaced by a teacher with no background in the work but who immediately earned the respect and trust of the pupils, partly because of his grasp of the subject but also because he was perceived as a safe and fair person.

Irrespective of the dictates of the curriculum, good teachers who are 'in authority' because they are 'an authority' will facilitate learning for even the most disturbed pupils. Within a week my pupils were telling me that I had got the appointment right this time because, 'That man really listens to you.'

Similarly, one of the most successful teachers in our school who, strictly speaking, is regarded as unqualified, regularly attains a high proportion of A and B grades in examinations in art. She is so determined to pursue her subject that the children are engulfed by her enthusiasm and energy which seems to overcome their anxieties.

The Environment and Facilities

Although the real strength of Enborne Lodge lies in the quality and quantity of human resources, many visitors regard the physical resources as lavish. Unlike boarding schools for children whose families are wealthy, we regard our environment as compensatory with plenty of room for energetic boys to foster their interests.

The transition from an 18-acre country estate to a utilitarian institution for our pupils has required further modifications with the advent of the National Curriculum. Discrete curricular areas, for example, of home economics, mechanics, woodwork, rural science and the farm have had to be cut back by the strictures of the new curriculum. A balance has to be struck between the narrower curricular needs of the pupils and their need for ordinary domestic lives, as private and as uninstitutionalised as possible.

Public displays

We believe, however, that the environment of the school should truly reflect our pupils' achievements and their sense of worth. In this respect we uphold the virtues described in Professor Rutter et al's (1979) book *Fifteen Thousand Hours* and every available piece of wall space and notice boards are full of children's work publicly displayed and mounted as expertly as possible. Work from children at all stages of development is displayed and the care we take in mounting suggests the way in which we value it.

Many of our pupils come from barren inner city estates where their sense of alienation manifests itself in the vandalising of public property. Here it is different. We have never had a piece of work on display in public areas damaged. The sense of displayed work being sacrosanct is learnt quickly by a community pressure from other boys which functions like a process of osmosis. We lavish praise on all new work displayed. I have witnessed the most violent tantrums from new boys which leave the fragile pottery display in the vicinity totally undisturbed. The children soon model on the adults by decorating and personalising their own bedrooms with similar fastidiousness.

The Methodology/Techniques

Many of the techniques we employ are derived from the needs of the boys we admit to the school. In the past, boarding special schools were more likely to follow either 'corrective' or 'medical' models, with the latter informing the choice between psychodynamic theory or behaviourism. The pendulum has now swung away from these and greater emphasis is placed on the work of cognitive theorists and focuses more on the child's learning deficits.

Pendulums have a habit of swinging back, however, and it may be that we will have to look again at whether the National Curriculum, when its shape is finally resolved, really requires redesigning to meet the needs of disturbed children.

Key universals

As described earlier, some of the key universals in describing our pupils centre around their poor self-esteem, their confused self-image and their learning difficulties. In our school, although the population comprises boys of above-average intelligence, the last of these is nearly always a concomitant component because of our pupils' previous patchy history of learning and often poor attendance or lengthy spells of suspension or exclusion.

At the point of contact with us, the family and the child are usually despairing. The child has often been excluded from school and therefore, apart from small amounts of home tuition if he is lucky, spends longer than usual reacting badly with family members or getting into trouble in the home environment. The assessment process leading to a statement can often take many months. When a special school is suggested, the family fears ostracism and stigmatisation and if a boarding special school is suggested they often carry an additional burden of guilt and the possibility of separation.

Even if the child is managing to sustain a place at school, teachers are torn between their need for relief from the problem, especially if the child is becoming increasingly hostile or defiant, and their own sense of inadequacy and professional guilt at not being able to contain either the child or their own feelings. It is at this point as well that the child falls behind the National Curriculum prescribed for his peers and further exacerbates our problems when we finally intervene.

Interview Day

A critical point is reached, then, when the child and his family make contact with the school on the day of interview. We have evolved a pattern of arranging this important day which takes into account the previous problems, addresses the current anxieties and sets out the ground rules clearly for our future work with the child.

The Contract

I cannot stress too much the importance of this day during which a 'contract' is made with all parties in which we as a school guarantee success in return for a proper commitment from the boy and his family. Sometimes, during a boy's time with us when the demands and expectations we make about his work and behaviour become too challenging for him, we refer back to those promises and remind ourselves what was negotiated.

When we ask pupils and their families at the beginning of the Interview Day what worries them most, the boy's answer is most commonly centred around the other pupils and 'what they are like', while the parents focus more on the possibility of 'getting a good enough education' for their son. It is explained that three things must happen before we offer a place at the school.

1. We as a school have to agree that we can meet the boy's needs as described in the statement or perceived by us on the day of interview.
2. The family must agree to work consistently with the school and to support the placement and its demands on them wholeheartedly.
3. The boy has to clearly say that he wants to come to the school.

To achieve the last two is often easy because the school is attractive and well-resourced and the pupils already here readily welcome a newcomer, look after him and spend time with him away from adults for part of the day. Creating an air of civility and order alleviates the anxieties of the parents and it would be easy for this process to be seductive. Our task, however, is to understand some of the family dynamics and assess carefully the child's learning needs.

To explain this I need to set out the rationale on which our work is based and describe some key features.

Structure and Autonomy
Disturbed and difficult children often lead disordered and chaotic lives and have developed few internal controls. Moreover, their inability to cope with the demands of ordinary schooling and their parents' often inadequate ways of dealing with them out of school is a frequent concomitant of their need to learn and live in a consistent total environment.

Pattern and routine
Most of our pupils welcome adults imposing a pattern and a routine on both their learning programmes and daily lives. Structure cannot be an end in itself, for that would lead to the creation of institutionalised automita. Our aim must be to produce at the end of his school-days a young adult who is happy and autonomous.

Early on the children are afraid of the anarchy of their own lives. Disturbed children are often frightened by the turbulence and power of their own emotions, and have an urgent need to feel safe and contained. Some children are withdrawn and phobic and need adult protection in the early years from their own fears; others have a history of disruption and violence. The structure of the school provides the security that curbs aggression by redirecting it onto worthwhile pursuits. The development of rapport and collaborative techniques ensure a calm, rational atmosphere in which the anxiety of both the adult and the child are diminished.

Collaboration and Incorporation
Collaboration involves the pupil feeling part of his own rehabilitation. Despite their obvious symptoms, our pupils are usually aware of their need for help with their learning problems and know the ways in which they differ from their peers. They are prepared to collaborate with any adult who offers to help them sincerely, but they also require to feel that the joint enterprise is paying off in terms of their own happiness and enhanced self-esteem.

Translated into practices at this school, our displays of children's work and the way they proudly wear badges for sporting achievements on their tracksuits clearly involve the enhancement of self-image and self-esteem. At every moment, during our work, we are aware that we cannot help a child make progress unless they are motivated to do so.

89

Shared Responsibility

An example of this is the way we allow boys to have a say in the running of their own affairs, particularly as they get older. Our school meetings often centre around the reports of various 'committees' that the boys have formed. These committees are freely elected by the pupils, occasionally have staff representatives and always must have some representation from junior boys.

Committees which run the boys' clubroom or organise their discos are clearly ones which are self-motivating, but the skills and practices involved in struggling to make rational arrangements from a wealth of conflicting opinion is translated directly to other areas by which, at first sight, the pupils would seem less motivated. For instance, their clothing committee and their catering committee give them a sense of involvement with affairs that concern their domestic lives directly and help prevent the sense that adults are either always making decisions for them or taking the responsibility away from them.

Rules and Respect

The school has literally hundreds of codified rules which are always explained in detail to the pupils. In essence these are derived from two principals — respect for people and respect for other people's property. Boys are encouraged to take on the complicated task of persuading us to fairly modify old rules or make new ones in areas which are of direct interest to their lives in the community.

There is some conflict between these collaborative processes, which are intrinsically valuable for our population, and the imposition of learning which is explicit in the National Curriculum. Although much learning at Enborne Lodge is directed by the teachers, the pupils are often more motivated by their own agenda. For instance, in the past technology (in its earlier incarnation as woodwork and metalwork) was often best taught by the children choosing the artefacts they wanted to make themselves and learning the techniques incidentally. A boy who was hoping to proudly take home a table or other piece of furniture was much more likely to be motivated by the thought of this, than is the case now where the techniques seem to be prescribed by the curriculum. We are forced to explain simply that, like Health and Safety and medical requirements, it is the law acting on all of us that determines what the pupils learn and the teachers teach.

Assessing Pupils' Needs

A vital component of the Interview Day is our own assessment of the child's learning difficulties and needs. Despite the information contained in assessment papers, we find that the direct interaction between the prospective pupil and his teacher in the context of his prospective classroom gives us a much clearer picture of previous gaps in learning and faulty learning strategies as well as areas of strength.

The child is assessed by the experienced Reception Unit teacher who has two main areas of concern. The first addresses the learning strategies of the boy. The second judges whether his inclusion in the class will lead to a balanced peer group in the school. What the teacher is looking at in respect of the first of these is not so much what the boy has learned but how he approaches a task. He or she is trying to gauge what is open to change and how much the boy is committed to engage in the task.

Most of our pupils on Interview Day are fearful and anxious, but this is not taken as a negative indicator because the real question that is being asked is, 'Is the child motivated enough or determined, at any level, to overcome previous difficulties?'

Many of the behavioural components of faulty learning strategies correlate with other facets of the child's functioning. For example, stubborn behaviour indicates the child's resistance to new learning; lying and cheating and obsessional behaviour all reflect how the child has previously attempted to deal with his learning difficulties.

Initiating Change

Collaboration in the educational process starts at this point. As unthreateningly as possible, the pupil is encouraged to both acknowledge his learning difficulties as well as to proffer reasons for them honestly. Part of our 'educational promise' is that we let the boy know that he is not alone in these difficulties and by pointing to the success of others like him, show that we both understand and can help.

Facing the challenge

We also, quite uncompromisingly, let him know his responsibilities and the elements of challenge involved that he must face if we are to help him overcome his difficulties. For instance, the child must know unequivocally that all the seductive parts of school life that he will enjoy are available to him on completion of his quota of school work.

Lesson time, the pupil is told, is not negotiable, nor will we relax our demand that during this time he must satisfactorily complete his side of the 'bargain'. Often with young children, or children who are not mature enough to keep their promises, this has to be reinforced early during their stay with us. If at any other stage a child seems to be falling short of the promises he makes at interview, a more formal contract is agreed between the pupil and the school. Always the binding force on the child is that he wishes to remain at the school.

Negotiation

This collaboration continues throughout a boy's time with us. Every boy must enter a self-reporting section on his school report and both review his own progress and set, jointly with his teachers, targets for the future. Older boys engaging in an often exhausting social life outside the school must negotiate to their teachers' satisfaction their revision time before examinations and, more rarely, senior boys are required to give up part of their weekends if their school work demands extra time.

The exact form of negotiation depends on the child's personality and his motivation, but generally all this is possible because the 'pay-off' is great enough to sustain the original intention. Of course, for some of our very youngest children the implications and consequences of their initial 'promise' are not always realistic and their collaboration is modified from time to time. In general it is the quality of relationship we establish with the children which is the determining factor. Ultimately the quality of life and stimulation that school can give them is the reward for following our instruction.

To understand the way we cope with the learning needs of the children, I should describe the structure of the formal part of the teaching process.

Induction

The most crucial phase of learning for pupils is when they first enter the school. This may be at any time during the academic year. Boys are nearly always placed first in the Reception Unit, except very occasionally when they would be much older than their peers there. Our experience is that when this happens they miss out a key component in the process of remediation both socially and educationally and do not develop an early dependence on the school experienced by others and which leads to independence later on.

The Reception Unit

The Reception Unit underpins everything we do in the school for pupils and acts as an induction to the community, as a place where boys, sometimes for the first time in their lives, learn to trust sufficiently to confide and discuss their problems. At this point they begin to tackle the educational and social deficits that they arrive with. Boys usually spend a year in the Unit but, if they are very young when they come (nine or ten), or have more intractable learning difficulties, they may remain between one or two more academic years there.

The peer group

The Unit, unlike the rest of the school, has the assistance of a support teacher and can take up to 12 boys at different social, emotional and educational stages. It is from here that a peer group of children is formed which travels through the school in groups of six or eight up to Year 11 and sometimes beyond to further education.

Clearly the demands of this group require a teacher of exceptional talents who is able to deal with a large chunk of the core curriculum as well as manage individual programmes which cater for specific learning difficulties, assessment and the crucial forging of a coherent group who learn the expectations of the school and are taught to facilitate each other's emotional development.

As I explained earlier, the National Curriculum has made this task both easier and more difficult for us. Easier because there is in theory a progression expected of every pupil by the time they come to us; harder because of the very nature of our pupils' previous school histories, with their interruptions caused by poor attendance, lack of engagement, and suspensions and exclusions. This, together with the often inordinate delays in the statementing process, means that even our brightest pupils are unsynchronized in their learning with their peers in mainstream.

In addition, the very nature of an imposed curriculum, as we shall see later, does carry the risk that for a talented teacher faced with a pupil with enormous learning deficits, some of the most imaginative ways of helping him are circumscribed or even precluded.

Case Studies

I can illustrate these points with some case histories.

Duncan

Duncan had been 18 months out of school when he was referred to us. He came from a family with a history of drug dependency who were in poor physical health and depressed. The family members communicated badly with each other and there were many 'family secrets'.

Prior to the National Curriculum, Duncan would have had a syllabus tailor-made to facilitate specific help. He would have been given learning materials designed to

93

'open up' and intervene in the areas of difficulties for him and topics would have been introduced to trigger these focal problems and to help him re-frame some of his ideas, even to the point of finding specific source materials that focused on secrets.

Under the injunctions of the National Curriculum, Duncan's gaps in knowledge must be papered over as best we can and, because of the time he has spent out of school, his assessment is inordinately rushed while we all try to help him catch up.

Arthur

Arthur was a child whose young mother died when he was five. She had refused her medication and had 'chosen' to die rather than be crippled for life from a rare disease. Arthur had a family who tried to care for him but also recognised that, although he was bereaved, he had been spoiled by his mother in her last year. Prior to coming to us no one had addressed the issues surrounding his mother's death with Arthur.

Arthur is bright, angry that he was left alone and emotionally desperate for a parent. At first sight it would appear that, were we to follow the National Curriculum guidelines, it would allow Arthur no space to explore these powerful feelings. In creative writing, for instance, it is demanded that pupils show 'an awareness of audience'. Yet Arthur constantly uses any theme to reveal aspects of his feelings of deliberate abandonment by his mother. If Arthur was strictly kept on task it would be at the expense of reworking those experiences.

In the case of Arthur our skilled Reception Unit teacher uses the National Curriculum in a way which best addresses his, and other pupils', emotional *and* academic needs.

For instance, early in their time in the Unit the pupils study biography and write autobiographies. This conforms to the National Curriculum requirements but provides the pupils with a safe vehicle for talking about their own experiences and emotions which can be re-framed with hindsight and help the child to come to terms with his current emotional state.

So when Arthur covered a pre-twentieth century literature requirement, he wrote about *Gulliver's Travels* from the point of view of a Lilliputian but personalised the account to talk about his own family. The teacher gently moved him on to address the subject in a way which allowed Arthur to write about his mother but also to fulfil the attainment target in an integrated way.

Peter

Peter was rejected at an early age by his father who was disappointed in him. He now has very poor self-esteem and his self-image is that of a victim. This has become a self-fulfilling prophesy in his relationships where he causes other to dominate him. He is intellectually bright and his professional mother, living apart from his father, has tried school after school to help Peter with his education. All these attempts failed to help Peter, who lives in a private world and has idiosyncratic ways of learning.

He was referred to us at the age of 13 and had completely missed out on Key Stage 2. Prior to the new curriculum we would have felt free to set out a new chronology of learning for Peter. Now we are obliged to press ahead while recognising that he must manage without this stage. This might entail many of his conceptual links being lost and his lack of initiation into modes of thought involved in, say, geography or history would impede his progress.

The new history curriculum, for instance, does not permit a Key Stage 3 pupil to parallel his own history with that of the world's. Peter has missed this component, so the teacher enables him to cover this area in his English work by combining the demands of the attainment targets in English while using history tests.

Peter now has a better sense of his own personal history and his place in the world and his prognosis for success in future external examinations is now brighter. Here, as in other aspects of special education, the curriculum can always be used as a therapeutic tool providing chaotic, disorganised lives with a more ordered sense of personal and interpersonal reality and fit.

Late Referrals

The problem in recent years has been exacerbated by the marked tendency for children to be referred to us later than we would like. In the past it was always best for a child with residential EBD needs to be presented to us at secondary transfer, partly because this made the transition more natural and partly because this gave us more time to succeed. There were always some children whom good primary schools struggled to support in their own communities and who then transferred to secondary schools where the process of referral did not begin in earnest until the end of their first year (Year 7). We were then faced with a young adolescent whose problems were less malleable and more severe.

The well-intentioned current belief that children are best managed in their own communities and the resourcing difficulties experienced by many LEAs often prevent our help being made available at the optimum time. Furthermore, it often means that even when our pupils make accelerated progress, if they enter our Reception Unit at 13 they are unlikely to have completed a two-year GCSE course until they are 17.

Progress Through School

Once pupils leave our Reception Unit they move to our second and third classes which completes their progress through Key Stage 3. The general tendency in the school is to move children from dependency to independence. This process is mirrored in the organisation of the curriculum for pupils at this stage of learning.

We characterise the work in these intermediate classes as 'primary style, secondary content' which reflects the responsibility that a form teacher for these groups has in delivering 50 per cent of the core curriculum and working as the continuous figure, analogous to the 'key worker' in a child care context. The teachers take responsibility for the children in their classes and act as pivotal adults communicating with other staff and the child about his needs. Those same teachers offer their specialisms to older pupils preparing for examinations.

At the end of Key Stage 3 pupils choose their 'options' for the two-year period in Years 10 and 11, leading to examinations. Previously, the collaborative style of the school was reflected in the way this offer was made and in many ways the timetable became client-led. Nowadays, of course, the National Curriculum dictates much of this and pupils have less freedom of choice.

At the end of Year 11 our pupils have generally acquired enough good GCSEs to be offered tertiary phase places at FE in vocational subjects or even A-level.

At this point the choice, following careful careers advice and taking into account their residual social and emotional needs, revolves around whether they leave to study at home or remain with us for the tertiary phase. If he remains at Enborne Lodge, a pupil's contract is renegotiated. We provide a flat and his life becomes increasingly independent of the rest of the community. The issues now are more concerned with the freedoms a boy may acquire in return for the responsibilities involved in successfully managing the independent living units.

An Evaluation of the National Curriculum

There is a remarkable degree of unanimity amongst the teaching staff about the merits and constraints of the National Curriculum compared to the curriculum we had devised for ourselves prior to the time that the 1988 Education Act's effects were filtering through. We had by then started to take in groups of brighter disturbed boys than hitherto and, if the acid test of our system was examination success, then we felt that our broad curriculum leading to an average of seven or eight GCSE passes with average grades was vindicated.

League tables

We wonder about the effects of the National Curriculum on self-esteem if our population was less bright and it became apparent that the final levels achieved fell below national averages. The concomitant of the curriculum insisted upon by the government is the publishing of 'league tables'. At Enborne Lodge these act as a confirmation of our pupils' achievement but elsewhere, with a different population, tables with zero ratings for academic success may be felt acutely by institutions where nonetheless much good work has gone on.

Offering structure

We feel that the National Curriculum for our boys identifies their similarities with the population in mainstream rather than making them feel inferior. We also think it offers a structure and acts as an *aide-mémoire* for our teachers in checking that our own syllabuses are properly initiating children into appropriate modes of thought. It also, because it is structured, allows pupils who ideally we would like to understand the intrinsic value of education, to latch on more easily to the extrinsic merits of 'getting qualifications' or 'going on to FE'. For teachers who are less confident there might also be a comfort in introducing elements of the curriculum because, 'the government or the law says so'.

For talented teachers or teachers with multiple skills, the reverse is true. They may feel restricted by the National Curriculum. I would cite art, music and PE as areas in this school where that is particularly the case. Our music teacher, for instance, not only has keyboard and woodwind skills but also makes use of percussion, synthesizers, composing and singing. Similarly, in art, painting, pottery, textiles, screen-printing, three-dimensional work and life drawings are a lot to be crammed into the pint-pot of the National Curriculum Attainment Targets. In a school where boys traditionally excel in County and even National Championships in a wide range of sports, the curriculum for PE is very limiting.

Individualised learning

There is also a sense in which the National Curriculum, primarily designed for use in mainstream for larger groups, is less appropriate when applied to the sort of individualised learning that goes on here, where small group teaching is one of the reasons children are referred to us in the first place. It also, as I have alluded to earlier in the chapter, cuts across the premium we place on children taking responsibility for, and collaborating in, their own learning. The sense that the National Curriculum is prescriptive and imposed on the pupils from outside school makes it more difficult to pursue individual talents with our children. Given the nature of this community and the poor parenting experienced by many of our pupils, there is a much greater urgency for them to leave us as independent and equipped for the world as possible. This is because often they are not supported as well by their families and are required or desire to leave their family home sooner than most young adults. This, allied to their slower rate of maturation, means that programmes of Lifeskills, Health and Sex Education, Parentcraft, Work Experience and the other components of our 'Leavers' Programme' become of vital importance to them. Home economics, for example, is being squeezed out of the curriculum in many schools, but pupils desperately need to know how to cook and understand the elements of a food and nutrition course.

Pressure of time

We can retrieve some of these losses because we have a curriculum which extends outside of the formal school day. However, many issues of emotional and social importance to our pupils stem directly from things they are learning in the classroom and are more properly addressed there, if we only had more time. Pressure of time and the narrower confines of the National Curriculum also cut into some of the critical areas that we have previously regarded as vital to our pupils.

We used to afford the luxury of half an hour's reading time every morning and, of course, counselling and group sessions and individual therapy have to now be more strictly rationed. We also feel that the nature of these pupils' learning styles demands a balance between academic and practical subjects. There is an intrinsic value in allotting more time to more vigorous pursuits. Similarly, some personal projects which have a therapeutic value and which are directly related to helping a child come to terms with some of his emotional difficulties are now more difficult to find the time and the space for.

Case Studies of School Leavers

Some case histories of leavers illustrate these points.

Gerald

Gerald was a boy brought up by his grandparents following the long-term hospitalisation of his mother with a psychiatric disorder. He had an IQ in the superior range and joined the school when he was 10. He had some specific learning difficulties but had an enormous interest in computers and computing. He was writing his own programmes by the time he was 13. He took his examinations and went on to FE in London, to study information technology.

While at school, Gerald joined the 'Break Dance' troupe and was part of a show performed to families on Open Day. Gerald now has a successful career not as a computer programmer but as a dancer.

Donald

Donald had specific learning difficulties and found practical subjects more comfortable. He attained low average examination passes, but while at school he became the pupil with the most expertise in the technical side of drama. Although Donald's family lived in London, he went on from us to a college in Lancashire at the age of 16 to attend a technical drama course. He now freelances successfully as a sound and light technician.

Ralph

Ralph was abandoned by both his parents and brought up by his grandmother. He had the ability to attain average examination grades, but his prowess in athletics was his motivation to do well in order to pursue his talents in further education on a sport and leisure course. He broke a British Junior sprint record and went on a sports scholarship to the USA.

Adjustment versus qualifications

Many years ago, when similar schools worked in a therapeutic mode, we used to worry about the price paid for this in terms of the child's educational attainments. I think now we have to consider whether the educational model pays sufficient attention to all the emotional needs of the child. On balance, I would prefer that our pupils grew up adjusted rather than qualified. In the end, that is a higher order of attainment to enable them to integrate into life after school and their future relationships.

Evidence of Success

Criteria which point to the successful outcome of residential placements are notoriously elusive. Some indices for the success of our methods while the pupils are with us are more easily agreed. Empirically, our pupils always return from weekend leave and holidays; we have never formally excluded a boy; they all stay at least until their examinations and Records of Achievements are completed. We regularly attain the best examination results in our sector and have achieved unusual success in sport. In the last ten years, seven of our pupils have been representatives in the All England Athletic Championships, for example.

Impressionistically, visitors are stuck by the attractive damage-free environment and the civility and friendliness of pupils. The community is a safe environment for the boys. Bullying and violence are almost non-existent. The families of our pupils support us enthusiastically.

The extended community of the school is further cause for satisfaction and the frequent contact with former pupils, many of whom now have their own families, is a delight. It gives a sense of direction and hope to our younger pupils.

Current Issues, Future Developments

It is too early to assess the impact of the National Curriculum on the long-term future of schools like Enborne Lodge and, at the moment, there are too many other imponderables affecting mainstream and special education. Many features of the 1988 Education Act and the 1993 Education Act have a bearing on our sector. Currently there is a national debate about youngsters who are failed by the education system and become involved in truancy and delinquency. Exclusions from schools and the pressures on schools to compete in the 'marketplace' with their neighbours has created new realities for the school-aged population.

Opting out

Boarding special schools are now brought into line with their counterparts in mainstream education and can 'opt out' of LEA control or become non-maintained with their local authorities' blessing. This ought to enable them each to specialise more and to make a more distinctive offer in what, I believe, should be an organised rather than a competitive market.

The Dearing Report

In addition, the Dearing 'Final Report on the Review of the National Curriculum' should free special boarding schools from the restrictive constraints of the earlier versions. The curriculum can now be broadened to match more closely pupils' abilities and needs and be more relevant for the children we serve.

Successful reintegration

Special educational needs and the integrationist issues were addressed in 1981 following the Warnock Report. Baroness Warnock herself now concedes that some features enacted at that time will need re-examining. The government and interested professionals will soon need to grasp the nettle of special education, which is unco-ordinated and piecemeal and, at the moment, too much at the mercy of educational whims and financial constraints.

In this school we hope we have shown that the notion of successful reintegration into society for previously disturbed, damaged children with learning difficulties is an achievable concept.

References

Peters R S (1966) *Ethics and Education*, Allen and Unwin: London.
Rutter, Michael, Maughan, Barbara, Mortimore, Peter, and Ouston, Jane (1979) *Fifteen Thousand Hours*, Open Books: London.
Stott, Denis H (1978) *Helping Children with Learning Difficulties*, Ward Lock Educational.
Wilson, Mary and Evans, Mary (1980) Schools' Council Working Paper 65, *Education of Disturbed Pupils*, Methuen Educational: London.

PART THREE

MANAGING CURRICULUM IMPROVEMENT FOR CHILDREN WITH EMOTIONAL AND BEHAVIOURAL DIFFICULTIES

CHAPTER 6

Curriculum Liaison Between Special and Mainstream Schools

By Roy Lund

This chapter is concerned with examining the historical links between mainstream secondary schools and schools for children with emotional and behavioural difficulties (EBD schools).

On a curricular plane, these links centred on the development of Certificate of Secondary Education (CSE) courses, which later developed into the existing General Certificate of Secondary Education (GCSE) and Technical, Vocational and Educational Initiative (TVEI) courses. EBD schools were fully involved in the formation of local 'consortia' for the development of courses and there is considerable evidence that this was to the mutual benefit of both mainstream and EBD schools.

The Education Reform Act of 1988 introduced the National Curriculum and this was welcomed by most teachers in special schools, as a means of forming a recognised framework and continuum for the education of *all* children. Paradoxically, apart from involvement in initial National Curriculum training, teachers in EBD schools have not maintained close links with mainstream schools for the purposes of shared curriculum development. This is despite the fact that adverse reports from HMI (1989 (a) and 1989 (b)) criticised curriculum organisation and delivery in EBD schools. In fact, there is considerable evidence that EBD schools have drifted further away from mainstream schools since the Education Reform Act.

What *are* the issues in the development of appropriate curricula and how is the current organisation of EBD and mainstream schools affecting this process?

Curriculum Organisation in EBD Schools

At the time of the Schools' Council Survey of the 'Education of Disturbed Pupils' project, led by Mary Wilson and Mary Evans (1980), EBD schools paid little attention to curriculum development. They tended to focus on teaching basic skills, mainly in English and mathematics and in practical activities like art, pottery, craft, cookery, drama and games. These activities had a limited academic content and were thought to be all that the pupils could cope with. Furthermore, it was believed that such activities offered the opportunity for the children to come to terms with, and resolve, their emotional difficulties.

The curriculum on offer was practical and hands-on and was often delivered by means of a project or topic-based approach; it was essentially child-centred. This style of curriculum organisation led easily to the incorporation of TVEI and Mode 3 CSE examination courses, which were at this time being developed by mainstream schools.

Co-operation between EBD Schools and Mainstream Schools Prior to the Introduction of the National Curriculum

EBD schools have traditionally liaised with mainstream schools for three reasons: in order to facilitate the transfer of pupils from one institution to another; for 'social' reasons; or for co-operation in various teaching and learning initiatives, like TVEI.

EBD schools developed links with mainstream schools for the development of CSE and, later, GCSE courses and became members of TVEI consortia. For example, the Northamptonshire *TVEI Special Schools Handbook 1988/89* highlights the way in which the county's two EBD secondary day schools were linking courses with colleges of FE and with 'link' comprehensive schools within their TVEI consortia (Northamptonshire CC 1988). One of these link comprehensive schools had gone so far as to appoint a member of staff as a 'liaison teacher'.

At the same time, one of the Northamptonshire EBD schools was developing informal links with mainstream subject departments in various schools. The idea was that each subject co-ordinator from the EBD school would link with a local comprehensive school subject department. At first, it was hoped that this would be with *all* the departments in the link comprehensive school, but it soon became apparent that certain departments were more sympathetic, and more favourably organised in terms of their potential co-operation, than others. In practice, therefore, the EBD school subject co-ordinators found sympathetic departments from a total of four different local comprehensive schools.

The main factor which these sympathetic departments had in common seemed to be a relatively child-centred approach. The ways in which they were working were more in harmony with the methods of teaching and learning outlined later on in this chapter as being appropriate for children with EBD. The heads of department involved were leaders in the development of appropriate curricula for all pupils, regardless of difficulty or special educational need.

At the same time, the mainstream schools in question were developing whole-school approaches to collaborative curriculum development, in which the *positive* management of behaviour was made a priority.

Throughout the process of forming links, the Local Education Authorities' Advisory Services played a key role. The advisors were involved in the appointment of heads of department and had advised and assisted in the setting up and development of courses. They also put like-minded progressive teachers in touch with each other: 'Why don't you talk to so and so?' often became the introduction to worthwhile collaborative work and this was particularly useful to the small EBD schools.

The advantages to the EBD school were:

- access to the latest developments in the teaching of particular subjects;
- an opportunity to develop and maintain professional skills with other like-minded specialists;
- a chance to develop Mode 3 CSE (and later GCSE) courses which suited pupils with emotional and behavioural difficulties.

The advantages to the mainstream schools were:

- a fresh insight into ensuring relevance, as far as curriculum content was concerned;
- help from specialist teachers in developing appropriate teaching methods for pupils with behavioural difficulties.

The relationship between the EBD school and the link comprehensives became mutually supportive in respect of issues such as pastoral care, personal and social education, and behaviour management policy.

107

Unfortunately, such links between mainstream and special schools do not appear to be common. *Joining Forces - A Study of Links Between Special and Ordinary Schools* (Jowett et al, 1988), the report of a research study promoted by the National Council for Educational Research, examined links between the two before the introduction of the National Curriculum. Although the study found that informal links existed, of the kind found at the beginning of this section, they found very few links that could be described, even remotely, as co-operation over the curriculum.

Curriculum Support for Pupils in Mainstream Schools

A number of LEAs have centrally funded support services for children with EBD. These services are under increasing financial pressure and are becoming increasingly superficial, as the bulk of available funding is delegated to schools.

Where support teachers do not belong to a centrally managed support service, they are unco-ordinated and there are consequent difficulties for ongoing training and professional and career development. Support is usually pegged to a particular child, via a statement of special needs. This often leads to several children being allocated small amounts of teaching support, sometimes within the same school. This is obviously not an efficient use of resources; the support teacher, or assistant, becomes the child's 'minder' and there is less chance of the subject or class teacher being able to differentiate the curriculum for the child involved.

While the child's personal problems may well be at the root of their unacceptable behaviour, it is a failure in differentiation of the curriculum which leads to its perception by the child as irrelevant. Support teaching should, therefore, centre on identifying the needs of the child with EBD and enabling the subject or class teacher to organise the curriculum in order to make it relevant to that child.

The Changing Role of LEAs

While the National Curriculum has provided a framework of curricular entitlement for *all* children, whether pupils of special or mainstream schools, recent developments resulting from the Education Reform Act of 1993 have not proved so beneficial to small EBD schools.

Many secondary schools, particularly in certain areas, have opted out of LEA control and become grant maintained. This has meant that their funding has been removed from the LEAs' control. In addition, the bulk of the remaining LEA funding has been delegated to the schools in their area, leaving very little at the direct disposal of the LEAs.

This means, in practice, that it is no longer possible for the LEAs to *re-allocate* monies to cover 'special cases'. Often, a child with SEN, or a small special school, cannot receive unplanned extra help when it is needed. Small schools (and all EBD schools are small) do not have enough money to purchase the curriculum services they require.

At the same time, LEA advisors and inspectors no longer play a key role in the appointment of heads of department or consequently in the development of specific subject teaching. This particular way of keeping schools in touch and promoting liaison has gone.

The effects of Local Management of Special Schools (LMSS) on EBD schools have exacerbated their isolation from mainstream schools. This isolation is likely to be felt even more keenly by grant-maintained special schools.

The Advent of the National Curriculum

The National Curriculum has provided a common framework for all children in all kinds of schools. It has highlighted the concept of the entitlement of all children to a 'broad and balanced curriculum'. There is, therefore, a much greater need for staff in EBD schools to liaise with their mainstream colleagues, in order to ensure that there is a common approach to structuring the programmes of study of the National Curriculum.

Exclusions

Since the introduction of the National Curriculum, however, there has been an increase in the number of exclusions from mainstream schools. Evidence gathered by Stirling (1992) suggests that official figures for the number of children who are excluded in no way accurately reflect the true number. Stirling quotes a National Union of Teachers' survey, published in June 1992, which found that 'pupil exclusions had risen by 20 per cent in one year (1991)' and the Secondary Heads' Association, which found that 'a quarter of pupils excluded from school disappeared from the education system completely'. OFSTED, in their report *Education for Disaffected Pupils* (1993), gives a number of reasons for the increase in exclusions, but not one of them is concerned with the quality of the curriculum or its perceived relevance to the pupils!

There is evidence that the introduction of the National Curriculum, with its apparent emphasis on discrete subjects and the decline in non-academic courses such as TVEI, has led to the perception of lessons as 'boring and irrelevant', resulting in increasingly inappropriate behaviour and consequent exclusions.

The effect on curriculum organisation and delivery in EBD schools has also been marked. It is probably true that EBD schools are offering a broader and more balanced curriculum, but it is, at the same time, impossible for small schools, with limited numbers of staff, to completely cover the requirements of the National Curriculum, especially at secondary level.

Discrete subjects

It is also questionable whether the *way* in which the National Curriculum is being taught is relevant to the needs of children with emotional and behavioural difficulties. There is considerable evidence to suggest that EBD schools are teaching discrete subjects and that cross-curricular and topic work has been severely reduced. There is also anecdotal evidence that pupils in EBD schools, having failed in the subject-oriented curriculum in mainstream schools, are rejecting more of the same in EBD schools. Teachers are complaining of the 'impossibility' of delivering the full National Curriculum and there is a general feeling that, if only the National Curriculum would go away, everything would be alright again.

In summary, the advent of the National Curriculum seems to have led to a discrete subject teaching approach in both mainstream and EBD schools, and an abandoning of courses such as TVEI, which appeared to have been perceived as relevant to pupils with behavioural difficulties and thus motivated their learning. Whether teachers in EBD or mainstream schools like it or not, however, the National Curriculum is here to stay and is, in fact, a valuable framework for continuity between the various settings in which children with emotional and behavioural difficulties might find themselves.

The Value of Increased Links Between Mainstream and EBD Schools

In the same way that effective methods of curriculum organisation and delivery in EBD schools pioneered courses which were perceived as relevant to pupils with behavioural difficulties in mainstream schools prior to the introduction of the National Curriculum, there could now be some benefit to mainstream schools from the way in which EBD schools are organising teaching and learning within the National Curriculum. The problem is, as has already been noted, that most EBD schools appear to have, at least temporarily, abandoned their traditional approaches which have a proven record of effectiveness. They obviously need to redevelop these techniques in relation to the National Curriculum.

At the same time, it is difficult to imagine how EBD schools can develop effective courses for themselves without help and support from their colleagues in mainstream schools, who are working to a greater balance and breadth and who have access to greater resources.

Teachers within the whole area of behavioural difficulties are feeling considerable stress in rationalising what they perceive to be good practice in teaching and learning for children with EBD and what they perceive to be the formal, subject-centred demands of the National Curriculum. As a result, they are feeling de-skilled. It is necessary to go back to first principles to examine just what constitutes good practice in EBD curriculum development and delivery, and to discuss the potential co-operation between mainstream and EBD schools in this process.

Children with EBD as Learners

If children with emotional and behavioural difficulties have anything in common with one another, it is the experience of failure in personal relationships and in learning. It is therefore important to ensure that all teaching and learning reinforces self-esteem, by ensuring success. It follows that the relationship between teachers and pupils in the learning situation can be an important vehicle for enabling the pupils to come to terms with their failure in personal relationships.

Self-esteem can be enhanced by celebrating achievement, not only in learning but also in the pupil/teacher relationship and in the area of co-operation between pupils. Mainstream schools, particularly at secondary phase, have historically not been very good at assessing work positively and celebrating achievement.

Building on success

Such children are also often hostile to new learning experiences and so need to have their programmes of study based on previous successful experiences; *success needs to build on success.* They often have a short attention span and therefore need *a wide variety of learning materials* and to experience learning through *a wide range of approaches.* They find great difficulty in dealing with abstract concepts, especially those outside the here and now; *all learning, therefore, needs to be concrete — practical and hands-on.* Topics, or cross-curricular themes, can be used to reinforce success and to give relevance to various concepts.

Children who are experiencing difficulties tend to perceive the world through their own immediate feelings and concerns; *feedback must therefore also be immediate and positive and must be perceived as personally relevant.* This has implications for co-operative group work, which such children find particularly difficult. They are sometimes so bound up in their own feelings and difficulties that they are unable to

111

concentrate on any form of learning; *the skilled teacher knows the right moment to change tack and to try a different approach.*

Above all, children with EBD take much longer than other children to do the same amount of work; *they need time.*

In summary, the main characteristics of differentiation of the curriculum for pupils with emotional and behavioural difficulties are:

Curriculum content
- Materials must be organised in a way which guarantees success.
- A variety of materials is required, to keep their attention.

The process of teaching and learning
- There should be a wide range of approaches, reinforced by topic work or cross-curricular themes.
- Learning should be practical and hands-on.
- Teaching should be child-centred and relevant to the child as a person, as well as a learner.

Curriculum Organisation

The primary, and most difficult, task of any EBD school today is to present the curriculum in a way which is seen as relevant by the pupils, but which, nevertheless, offers access to the National Curriculum and to external qualifications, both academic and vocational.

There is considerable anecdotal evidence at present to suggest that this is not happening. EBD schools have, by and large, reverted to a subject-oriented approach which, as has already been pointed out, is often rejected by pupils as being irrelevant to their needs.

There are, obviously, certain experiences and skills which can only be taught within subjects, more so as pupils get older and need to relate to external examinations. The fundamental problem is how to present the curriculum through a combination of project work, subject teaching and cross-curricular themes, while still fulfilling the requirements of the National Curriculum. The answer lies with the *subject co-ordinator,* who can ensure harmony between what appear to be conflicting interests in the following ways:

1. Assessing the individual learning needs of each pupil in their subject area, in relation to their behavioural difficulties.

2. Auditing all project work, subject teaching and cross-curricular themes, to ensure that the National Curriculum is covered and that each pupil has access to it.
3. Maintaining a two-way link with a mainstream school's subject department, for the purposes of keeping in touch with best mainstream practice and shared curriculum development.
4. Developing appropriate examination courses in co-operation with their mainstream subject department.
5. Covering their subject area in the pupils' Records of Achievement.

The process for this organisation within the EBD school could be via:

- shared staff planning for co-operative projects and cross-curricular themes;
- ongoing schemes of work, audited by co-ordinators against the requirements of the National Curriculum and modified accordingly;
- ongoing group and individual timetables, split into half-term and weekly blocks;
- individual targets, planned with each pupil, for and within each lesson;
- the assessment and celebration of achievement;
- ongoing records of work covered within each subject at each key stage.

Practical difficulties

In practice, of course, there are all kinds of practical difficulties involved in such an approach.

- Most schools for children with EBD are small and, therefore, have a limited range of subject teaching skills within their staffs.
- EBD schools are often cross-phase, thereby emphasising their smallness.
- Teachers tend to be appointed to EBD schools because of their skills in interpersonal relationships, not specifically for their subject teaching skills.
- Specialist practical facilities have been lacking in EBD schools, especially in the areas of science and technology.

These practical difficulties have led to great stresses amongst EBD school staff; teachers often have to take responsibility for more than one subject area and their personal relationships are suffering, due to the pressure of subject organisation and delivery.

Take, as an example, ten teachers (including the head and deputy) in a 50-pupil EBD school. If one of the teachers is attending a course, one is off sick, one is talking to a parent who has called in and one or two are dealing with a violent temper outburst from one of the children, *the school cannot function within the timetable that has been developed.*

While two-way links with mainstream schools can offer a positive way forward in enabling teachers to develop their skills, these practical difficulties, which make such demands on their time, have effectively confined EBD teachers to their own small schools.

How can these practical difficulties be resolved?

Towards a New Model of Co-operation Between EBD and Mainstream Schools

The first task of the EBD school is to establish the kind of curriculum organisation already outlined. This may not be entirely effective at first, because any small school will only be able to implement such an organisation superficially. It is, however, essential as a basis for co-operation with mainstream schools.

Opportunity to grow

What is then required is an opportunity for the special school to grow. At present, mainstream schools are having great difficulty in developing and delivering a curriculum which is perceived as relevant to their disaffected pupils. They are also having difficulties with certain pupils who are excluded and who are then not offered the kind of curriculum to which they are entitled (OFSTED 1993).

An informal survey of 18 Hertfordshire secondary schools, conducted as part of the preparation for this review, indicates that mainstream schools are concerned about the quality and level of support available to them for children with behavioural difficulties. The survey also highlighted the difficulties caused by the lengthy process of formal assessment under the Education Act 1981 (statementing) and the lack of a continuum of consultancy, support and resources for difficult pupils.

Levels of support

The headteachers of these schools have identified three levels of support in which they are interested.

Level 1

Support for subject/class teachers in mainstream schools, in order to help them organise their teaching and learning to meet the needs of pupils with EBD (mainly Years 7, 8 and 9).

Level 2

The withdrawal of individual pupils, in order to meet specific targets relating to their undesirable behaviour (mainly Years 7, 8 and 9).

Level 3

Groups of pupils whose behaviour is not likely to be appropriate for continuing placement in a mainstream school (likely permanent exclusions) (mainly Years 10 and 11).

It would be possible for EBD schools to provide support within Level 1 as 'outreach' and Level 2 as 'withdrawal' (for a set period) to an EBD site. Level 3 groups could be set up as Pupil Referral Units (PRUs), as outlined in the Education Act 1993 and managed as satellites by the EBD schools. Funding would need to be provided jointly by the LEA and mainstream schools, as fees paid to either maintained or grant maintained EBD schools.

The advantages of such a behaviour management service for mainstream schools would be:

- to enable each mainstream school to assess the needs of all pupils causing concern because of behavioural difficulties;
- to have appropriate packages of resources and support recommended, which would enable them to deal more effectively with these pupils, both in the long and short term;
- the provision of direct support teaching, where appropriate;
- the provision of a full programme of teaching, including the National Curriculum and external examination courses, for all pupil whose mainstream placements have irretrievably broken down.

The advantages for the EBD schools would be:

- earlier detection and assessment of potential pupils;
- a wider range of subject specialisation which could be used throughout the school and any satellite(s);
- increased access to mainstream departments for help in curriculum development;
- an improved training, professional and career development structure for teachers and support assistants.

A Possible Scenario

Representatives of the LEAs, local mainstream schools and EBD schools would meet to agree on a programme for reviewing and developing the new service. The agenda for such a meeting might run along the following lines:

1. Review of all resources, buildings, programmes and staff concerned with children with behavioural difficulties.
2. A proposal for the structure of the three levels of support previously outlined.
3. Detailed staffing proposals.

4. Budget requirements.
5. Agree funding required from LEAs and mainstream schools.
6. Trial period.
7. Review.

In practice, difficulty could be experienced in getting the scheme off the ground if mainstream schools did not agree, at least in principle, to 'opt in' to the proposals. Many mainstream schools increasingly see the LEA as being responsible for pupils they are unable, or unwilling, to teach. However, many LEAs are underwriting the initial costs of their advisory services and there is considerable evidence to suggest that schools are prepared to purchase such services.

There is a danger that such a scheme might run the risk of becoming a dumping ground for pupils which mainstream schools do not want. It would be necessary to demonstrate to them that *all* their concerns about pupils would be taken seriously. If a school wanted a pupil removed to a PRU, it would be counter-productive to the spirit of co-operation to refuse such a request. The scheme would probably begin by working in a reactive way, but become more proactive as trusting relationships developed between the EBD and mainstream schools involved.

Conclusions

Paradoxically, local authorities are likely to assume even greater responsibility for children with behavioural difficulties, while having fewer resources to provide services to deal with them. Meanwhile, EBD schools are struggling to develop appropriate teaching and learning strategies within the National Curriculum, because of their small size and failure to locate their work within the continuum of provision for children with behavioural difficulties.

The answer seems to lie in the development of a new role for EBD schools, as managers and providers of *services* for mainstream schools and for *all* children with emotional and behavioural difficulties, in partnership with LEAs and mainstream schools. It is only in this way that disaffected and excluded pupils can be provided with a continuum of curricular provision and thereby avoid social and academic isolation.

References
Jowett, et al (1988) *Joining Forces - A Study of Links Between Special and Ordinary Schools,* Falmer Press: London.
OFSTED report (1990/92) 'Education for Disaffected Pupils'.

CHAPTER 7

Improving Access to the Curriculum for Pupils with EBD in a Mainstream School: One Headteacher's Approach

By Paul Cooper

In this chapter an account is given of one headteacher's approach to the problem of raising academic and behavioural standards in a failing secondary school. A constant theme throughout this book has been the need to create circumstances in schools that enable vulnerable pupils to develop a positive sense of self in order to have the confidence to tackle the demands of the curriculum. This chapter shows how one headteacher works collaboratively with her staff in order to bring about the necessary changes in school structure.

The Valley School

The Valley Comprehensive School is located on a run-down council estate where there are high levels of unemployment and other social problems. The current headteacher, Ms Lincoln, took up her post in 1984, and was immediately struck by the picture of disaffection and failure that faced her. There was little sense of pupils having self-respect. Buildings were damaged and graffitied. To hear children run their school down, and run their teachers down as they did, was an eye-opener for her.

117

Furthermore, examination results were poor by local and national standards, there was a high level of truancy and a high delinquency rate among pupils. Unsurprisingly, staff morale was extremely low. They could see what they were doing was not successful. The teachers' main concern was with disruption in the classroom. They believed you did not really look for good examination results in a comprehensive school. Their expectations were very low.

Establishing a New Ethos

A great deal of care was taken by Ms Lincoln and her management team to introduce the changes in a way that took account of the staff needs and state of readiness. For example, one major reform involved the integration of pupils with special educational needs into the mainstream curriculum. This was staged over a period of five years, and feedback from staff made an important contribution to the rate of progress toward full integration. This process of staff consultation is an important theme which Ms Lincoln returns to often, and it reflects something of the overall ethos of the school that Ms Lincoln is attempting to build.

Mutual respect

At the heart of the new ethos is the importance of mutual respect among pupils and between pupils and teachers. Ms Lincoln is quite clear that while the curriculum is the main vehicle of opportunity for pupils, pupils will not make the best use of the opportunities offered without good-quality teacher-pupil relationships:

Initially the staff relationships with pupils were not satisfactory. Too often staff behaved in ways which conveyed the message: 'I am a teacher, you will respect me'. Ms Lincoln gradually had to change that to: 'I am a teacher, yes, but you are a pupil, and we demand equal respect of each other. And you can't swear at me if I'm not allowed to swear at you.'

Without these improvements in teacher–pupil relationships, the old antagonisms that existed between the two groups would continue to cause blockages in the lines of staff–pupil communication, and the level of collaboration and investment of effort, on which the new curriculum depended, would not be achieved.

Staff Training

The changes in staff ways of relating to pupils were achieved, according to Ms Lincoln, through a process of 'overt and covert' inservice training. The 'covert' training was training by example: the unobtrusive display of good practice. She keeps a very high profile in the school. She likes to let the staff see that she is doing what she is asking them to do. No matter what a child had done, she always tried to get through to the child, 'I don't hate you for doing this, but you've let me down with what you've done.' She found a tendency among staff to imply, 'you are stupid!' rather than, 'what a stupid thing to do!' She used to find staff knocking on her door too often, refusing to teach a particular child any more.

Staff workshops

This central theme of respect for persons is reflected in the 'overt' training also. Much of this training takes place in the regular whole-staff meetings, which take the form of workshops. A key feature of these meetings is staff participation.

The workshops are each organised around a question or problem which is generated from an issue of current concern in the school. Topics so far covered include:

- What makes a good school?
- The role of the form tutor: healing the pastoral academic divide.
- Devising a school environment development plan.
- Record keeping: what should they contain?
- Models of record keeping.
- 'What should be done if . . .?' Responding to problem behaviour in the school.
- Rewards for pupils.
- Public relations: the Valley School and the community.

The format of the meetings varies according to the topic, but the common pattern is for the meeting to commence with a presentation, in which a problem is stated and staff are briefed as to the task in hand, and then for staff to break off into small (six or seven staff) discussion groups. Outcomes of the small group discussions are recorded.

After the meeting these outcomes are collated by a member of the management team and a report is prepared which is distributed to staff. If further consultation or discussion is felt to be necessary, a second meeting may be called. Where topics arise out of the need for policy decisions to be made, the management decisions will be stated in the post-meeting report, with close reference to staff views expressed in the workshop, though not necessarily in agreement with views expressed.

Written reports

One important workshop, addressing the question 'what makes a good school?', touched on the issue of consultation procedures in the school, and received this reply in the written report, prepared by the head:

'Staff views were certainly divided as to the success of consultation procedures within the school, according to the comments made. I must, however, make it clear: in any school where I am head, decisions will be taken following consultation with you and after listening to a wide range of views. It will never be a participative form of government with the majority vote carrying the day or based on a Countesthorpe-type moot. The governors appointed me head with full approval of my style of management; that's what they wanted and that's the way it will be. I will listen to your opinions, always, but the fact that you don't always like the final decisions taken does *not* mean you have not been consulted or that it was only lip service being paid! My accountability is not only to the staff but to the whole community of which members of staff are certainly an important part. Through more frequent staff meetings I will have more opportunity of giving you feedback on why particular decisions, popular and unpopular, have been made.'

This statement also has to be considered in the context of a large group of responses from an earlier round of staff interviews conducted by the head:

'In the staff interviews I held in the summer term [1987] I received an overwhelming number of pleas from individual staff not to try and consult too widely, but to direct staff what to do. I was assured that staff would prefer to be told what to do, however unpalatable, and they felt that was what I was paid for!'

The important thing here, however, appears to be the fact that there is an active dialogue taking place, in which staff are able to make their feelings known and are given the right to expect a response. It is interesting to note that subsequent reports of meetings suggest that these complaints have not persisted.

Qualities of a good school

An examination of some of the workshop reports leaves the reader with the impression that there is, in fact, strong and effective process of staff consultation at work in the Valley School. The 1988 workshop, entitled 'What makes a good school?', exemplifies this point, marking, as it appears to have done, the starting point for many subsequent changes in the school. In this workshop, staff were asked to construct a list of qualities that characterise 'a good school'. They were then asked to consider the ways in which the Valley School matched up to these aspirations.

Finally, the staff were required to make some practical suggestions as to how the school might be brought closer to the ideal.

The first task generated a total of 20 qualities which, interestingly, reflect quite closely the values espoused by Ms Lincoln, indicating the commonality of purpose among the staff of the Valley School that was developing in 1988:

- strong head with a good sense of direction — obvious and effective leadership;
- pride in school;
- good resourcing level;
- caring community, where there is respect for people and property; quiet environment;
- desire to do well — a community where achievement in all spheres is encouraged;
- change managed sensitively with respect to the demands on staff;
- governors involved in the school;
- established disciplinary framework, help and support for new, probationary and supply staff;
- effective communications;
- good public image cultivated;
- stability – traditional values;
- educationally forward-thinking and innovative;
- good exam results;
- lack of graffiti, litter, damage;
- the school's policy about what it is attempting to do is clear and is kept updated; clearly stated common goals;
- good working relationships with other schools;
- able to take any visitor to any part of the school at any time;
- lots of extra-curricular activities;
- good atmosphere.

This list reinforces many of the points made by Ms Lincoln, particularly her concern to create a school where there is a positive co-operative atmosphere, which extends a wide range of opportunities to all pupils and engenders a sense of pride among those who are associated with the school. The item which refers to the need for sensitive handling of change in relation to staff needs is also interesting, as we have already seen this to be an important consideration among the management team at The Valley. The importance of pupils' self-esteem and pride in their achievements is further emphasised by a supplementary list, which relates specifically to the pupils of 'a good school'.

A good school is one where:

- pupils of all abilities are achieving set goals and achieving their potential;
- there is a good work ethic;
- pupils take responsibility for themselves;
- pupils have self-respect and respect for others;
- there is care taken of the environment, pride in the school, and a sense of belonging and identity;
- there is a good range of sports/leisure/extra-curricular activities;
- pupils have a sense of commitment and purpose;
- pupils are happy to be here; we would be happy for our own or friends' children to attend;
- pupils also behave well outside school;
- there are good sports results.

A further list relates to staff. A good school is one where:

- staff can practice their own specialities;
- staff are happy to work and morale is high;
- staff are professionals;
- staff are able to respond to pupils' individual needs;
- there is consistency and uniformity of standards for behaviour and discipline;
- staff, including supply staff, are respected;
- staff work as a team without excessive hierarchical structure;
- staff have a commitment to providing a curriculum for the whole ability range, believing in equality of opportunity for pupils of all abilities, and where curriculum support is available to bring out the best in pupils;
- relationships between staff and pupils are good.

In addition an important quality of 'a good school' is seen to be 'good relationships between school and parents'.

The school community

What comes across strongly from a consideration of these lists of qualities is the teachers' aspirations for a school which operates as a cohesive caring community, in which the members of the community — staff as well as pupils — are treated with respect and consideration for themselves as persons; where everyone has an opportunity for personal development, and is motivated to make a full contribution to the school community. In short, there seems to be little to choose between the list of qualities and the aspirations expressed by Ms Lincoln. Of course, not all of these qualities were identified by all of the groups; they are an amalgam of the lists generated by the small staff groups.

The workshop process can be seen as a means by which opinions and ideas are generated and shared with a wider audience. The act of dissemination, in itself, it could be argued, can be a motivating force for staff, by giving their individual views the status of publication. However, the sense of ownership and involvement that Ms Lincoln suggests as an important product of the workshops is more obviously attributable to the obvious and tangible outcomes that ensue from these meetings.

Current shortcomings

In the case of the 'what makes a good school' workshop, the staff groups produced a list of shortcomings which they felt the Valley School would have to address before it could be a 'good school'. These shortcomings included:

In relation to pupils
- the failure of the school to stretch its most able pupils;
- the low self-esteem felt by many pupils;
- the poor public image/low public status of the school;
- the failure of a minority of pupils (20 per cent - 25 per cent) to conform to behavioural expectations;
- the lack of consistency among staff in their behavioural expectations of pupils.

In relation to staff
- management ignoring majority staff views without adequate explanation;
- lack of a consistent code of staff expectations for pupil behaviour;
- realisation that a disciplinary approach to problem pupils is not always appropriate, but a lack of knowledge of how to cope with problems that may stem from pupils' personal difficulties;
- pressure of current climate and pace of change;
- lack of stability for pupils, caused by internal changes and externally imposed changes.

Once again, we find a strong degree of agreement between the staff perceptions recorded here, particularly those relating to pupils, and those expressed by Ms Lincoln. To some extent, these views act as an endorsement for measures that were already in motion, especially the new curriculum, which at that time was in its first year of operation. Other areas of concern, however, appear to have gained prominence as a result of this meeting and led to subsequent action.

Developments from workshops

It is impossible to detail all of the developments which appear to have grown out of this meeting, but it is possible to focus on a number of key strands which can be traced from this source. Firstly, the staff complaint about lack of explanation for management decisions which appeared to ignore majority staff opinion was met, on the basis of suggestions that were generated at the same workshop, with an increase in the frequency of whole-staff meetings, and the tabling on the agenda of space for the head to deliver more extensive explanations of decisions.

Secondly, the call for improvements in consistency of disciplinary standards and concern over pupil motivation led to further meetings which produced a disciplinary code and a school policy on rewards. The discipline code emerged partly from a workshop in which staff discussed approaches to a number of case studies of problem behaviour. The outcome of this was a policy statement which details the types of teacher response felt to be most appropriate to particular forms of problem behaviour, and sets out a clear pattern of referral for problems that require more input than the class teacher can supply.

As a result of the 'Rewards for pupils' workshop, a formal rewards system was introduced to publicly reward pupils, across the age and ability range, for their achievements in academic and other areas. The credit system also led to changes in the annual prize giving, to the extent that at the last prize day, one in four pupils were able to receive a prize for achievement of one kind or another.

One of the more complex problems was felt by staff to be that of the emotional and behavioural problems that some pupils exhibited. This was one problem which staff seemed to feel could not be easily dealt with within the school's existing provision. Centrally, staff felt they were not equipped with the expertise or, more particularly, the time to deal with the very real personal problems that a significant proportion of their pupils brought with them to school, and that often exploded in the classroom in the form of disruptive behaviour. The staff proposed a solution which involved the appointment of a professional counsellor for pupils. A year later, a half-time post for a school counsellor was created.

Consultation in management

These outcomes lend support to Ms Lincoln's claim that consultation plays an important role in her management style. There is also an indication of a firm basis for Ms Lincoln's claim that her staff possess a sense of ownership of and commitment to the school, partly as a result of their involvement in the changes facilitated by the workshop programme.

The nature of the changes themselves also reflects the sense of community and co-operation that is central to the ethos of the school, as is shown from an examination of the disciplinary code and the rewards policy. In these two policy areas we see clear evidence of an endeavour to create policy which provides a secure and stable framework within which individuals are clear as to expectations and responsibilities.

The Curriculum

The curriculum which was eventually put into place embodies many of the principles which run through staff thinking about the shortcomings of their school. Whereas the old curriculum was designed in an attempt to ape the local grammar schools, the new curriculum addressed more directly the needs of the Valley pupils. The core curriculum of ten subjects pre-empted almost exactly the subjects prescribed by the National Curriculum, and all pupils are required to take all of these subjects to GCSE level. In addition, at the end of Year 9, pupils are required to choose an additional subject. There is also a range of 'top up' options for pupils with sufficient space on their timetables.

The curriculum is strongly influenced by TVEI thinking, carrying an emphasis on coursework and industrial/technical/commercial studies and student-centred learning approaches, as well as the more traditional academic studies. The emphasis on coursework is shown by the fact that English, humanities, community studies, expressive arts, design and technology, French and German GCSEs are all awarded on the basis of 100 per cent coursework, while maths has a 50 per cent coursework component and science 45 per cent.

Modular approaches are also favoured, and there is a strong emphasis placed on giving pupils first-hand experience of real life situations and opportunities to reflect on their own situations and environment. One subject on the core course is community and industrial studies, which leads to the GCSE in social science. This course is based wholly on the study of the local community and its industry, and includes a two-week placement for each pupil with a local employer.

At the time of writing, the new curriculum was well underway at the Valley, and staff opinions were claimed by senior management to be very favourable toward it. There have been government-sponsored changes in the balance between coursework and final examination at GCSE, which will inevitably influence the curriculum. The impact of these and other changes is not known at the time of writing, but it seems fair to state that current government's emphasis on examinations and pencil and paper testing is not likely to favour the kind of student-centred approach adopted at the Valley School.

The thinking underlying the introduction of the new curriculum relates to the broader intentions of the new headteacher to overhaul the existing ethos of the school. The curriculum is seen as one, albeit centrally important, area in which the new ethos is reflected.

The new ethos is underpinned by four key principles which apply to both staff and pupils, and can be paraphrased in the following way:

1. the importance of respect for self and others;
2. the entitlement to experience success;
3. the availability of public praise and reward to all pupils;
4. the entitlement to be involved and to be heard.

The curriculum addresses numbers 2, 3 and 4 directly, and contributes to number 1 through its cumulative effects in combination with other school features, in a more general sense.

The Entitlement to Experience Success

The headteacher believes that the 'grammar school style' curriculum, which was in existence when she arrived at the school, presented a barrier to many of her pupils. The introduction courses with an emphasis on coursework introduced a much-needed element of flexibility into the learning programmes of all pupils.

Coursework provides opportunities for pupils to develop subject skills and confidence, by enabling pupils to improve their written work through the drafting process, under the guidance of teachers. Furthermore, the gradual accumulation of pieces of work which will count towards the final grade gives pupils a sense of progress and achievement, which is essential to the development of their self-esteem. Coursework also provides pupils with a wider range of choice than terminal examinations, and the opportunity to work on matters which are of interest to them in depth. Of equal importance to pupils, many of whom came from homes which are not conducive to the efficient completion of homework, is the way in which coursework deadlines can be made flexible.

Modular courses were also felt to provide flexibility, which enabled pupils to work towards short-term goals in a range of areas. Both the modular and the coursework system were felt to offer often unconfident and hesitant pupils the opportunity to develop their own interests and to experience success and achievement regularly.

An important innovation was the introduction of a social studies GCSE course, which focused on the study of the pupils' local environment. This, like the coursework options, was designed to give pupils a sense of the relevance of their school experience in their personal lives and that of their community, as well as fostering a sense of pride and ownership.

The Availability of Public Praise and Reward to All Pupils

It is important to stress that pupils are not only rewarded for their work in terms of GCSE results, though regular, thorough and prompt feedback for pupils' study assignments is seen as a central feature of school life. A system of weekly, half-termly and annual rewards is operated at the Valley School through subject departments and pastoral year groups. Pupils are able to gather reward and praise for a wide variety of achievements in curricular, social, sporting and other spheres. There is a finely graded progressive reward schedule which starts with commendation slips, on which the specific achievement is recorded, and progresses to more public forms of praise, including letters home to parents. Consistently praiseworthy behaviour is rewarded in half-termly assemblies, with a public citation and a certificate of commendation.

The Universal Right to Be Involved and to Be Heard

The curriculum provides many practical opportunities for pupils to discover, express and explore their own views. Modular and coursework assignments offer pupils opportunities to pursue their own interests and lend themselves to interactive teaching styles, which encourage pupils' active participation in lessons. This process is aided by the availability of curriculum support staff who are encouraged to focus their attention where it is immediately required in lessons, rather than concentrating on pupils formally declared to have learning or other difficulties, who will certainly not require individual attention all of the time. In these ways the curriculum feeds the development of pupils' self-image as active and competent learners who are able to take responsibility for their own learning.

Pupil council

The introduction of an elected pupil council with real power over a small budget is also seen as an important focus for pupil involvement in school life. This has grown out of a developing concern among staff to encourage pupils to engage in debating real issues. The work of the pupil council is encouraged to spill over into the formal curriculum where this is appropriate.

Curriculum Support Network

Of course, neither the modular system nor the emphasis on coursework would have had any positive impact without the establishment of a curriculum support network, which was designed to serve all pupils in mainstream classes, and not just those with special needs who are now fully integrated into the mainstream. While the core of the curriculum support faculty was provided by staff who had formerly worked in the MLD unit, mainstream staff are encouraged to develop support skills through INSET.

A further measure, designed to avert the possible marginalisation of the support network, is to insist that new staff who are appointed to the curriculum support faculty are able and willing to teach in the mainstream, and preferably up to A-level.

The Pastoral Academic Divide

The growing success of the school, which has recently been rewarded by an increased intake, cannot be attributed to the new curriculum alone. The curriculum stands at the centre of school life, but is in turn supported by a number of other measures which reflect and underpin the consistently pupil-centred values which the curriculum embodies. The pastoral system of the school has been realigned from its function as a disciplinary/crisis management centre into a pupil support service. Year heads are encouraged to work closely with subject departments and to take responsibility for collating an overview of pupils' academic progress, on the grounds that pupils' personal problems often first manifest themselves in the deterioration of their academic performance.

Similarly, the school recognises that academic dysfunctions, which can so easily lead to problems of disaffection, can sometimes be treated by adjustments in the learning environment or in teacher behaviour. The involvement of pastoral staff in the curriculum creates opportunities for such situations to be identified by an external figure, and for solutions to be sought at an early stage.

Discipline code

A second important support mechanism is provided by the discipline code, which provides teachers with a clear and concise set of procedures for dealing with disciplinary matters. The code is based on the principles of early, particularised and constructive intervention. The code divides disciplinary problems into 'minor', 'persistent' and 'urgent' categories. Minor matters are considered to fall within the ambit of the classroom teacher, while the other two categories cover those matters which are considered to fall outside this range, and require intervention at a department or senior management level.

Central to the discipline code is the importance of gathering evidence and the need to allow pupils to give their own accounts of incidents. Responses to disciplinary infringements are deliberately not codified, but are formulated in response to the problem in its particular context, and may take the form of measures as diverse as punishment (e.g. detention), adjustment of learning environment, liaison with parents, liaison with other agencies (e.g. psychological service) or advice to visit the school counsellor.

School counsellor

The school counsellor is a further support service which has been introduced into the school. The school employs a half-time counsellor whose role is to provide confidential counselling for pupils. The pupils are self-referring. The counselling process often leads to the initiation of specific measures for pupils (such as parental liaison, involvement of external agencies, provision of curricular support or liaison with particular staff). The general picture of common pupil concerns raised by counsellees also feeds into the general monitoring processes of the school, and where necessary is reflected in curricular changes.

Conclusion

In this chapter a brief account has been given of one mainstream school's attempts to improve the effectiveness of its services to its (often disaffected and disruptive) pupils. The provision of an appropriate curriculum is seen to be central to the process of improvement.

The original problems faced by the school were diagnosed in terms of disaffection bred from failure within an inappropriate curriculum. The new curriculum, and its attendant reforms, were designed to improve pupils' sense of self-worth through the experience of success and involvement in school life. The curriculum is underpinned by a recognition that pupils who have little experience or expectation of success require ongoing support in the form of staged, steadily paced and personally stimulating learning experiences, coupled with regular and positive feedback on their performance and attainment.

Pressure on pupils is diffused by the course and assessment structures, and their involvement is encouraged through the choice of content and manner of delivery. Furthermore, the curriculum is embedded within a school organisation which stresses the importance of personal support and care for pupils.

Finally, it should be pointed out that the research on which this chapter is based was carried out in 1991, before the National Curriculum had had any appreciable effect on secondary schools. Similarly, this also predates the government regulations which restrict coursework at GCSE to a maximum of 40 per cent of the final mark. While the National Curriculum, in terms of its attainment targets and programmes of study, had been welcomed by many teachers, the assessment arrangements would seem to threaten much of the good practice that has been outlined in this chapter.

Recent (and not so recent: e.g. Barnes, 1976) research suggests that teachers and pupils place a high value on teaching and learning activities which involve pupils in constructive and active ways in classroom events, and which encourage the importation of pupils' personal knowledge into the classroom context. Similarly, it has been argued that it is precisely such an environment, where pupils experience a sense of being valued, and where they experience genuine opportunities to achieve success in a climate of care and support, that is most conducive to the alleviation of emotional and behavioural difficulties.

While there is valid concern that the needs of EBD and other SEN pupils are sometimes in conflict with government education policy and thinking (e.g. the increasing tendency of the government to favour demotivating measures such as streaming by ability, depersonalised approaches such as whole-class teaching, and crude and threatening instruments such as terminal written tests), the evidence provided in this chapter and the others in this book is that creative, imaginative and dedicated teachers are able to meet these most vulnerable pupils' needs. It is hoped that the thinking and practices described in this book will help others to do likewise.

References

Barnes, D (1976) *From Communication to Curriculum,* Penguin: Harmondsworth.

Cooper, P (1992) 'Exploring pupils' perceptions of the effects of a residential school for children with EBD,' *Therapeutic Care and Education,* Vol. 10, No. 1 (pp. 22-36).

Cooper, P (1993) *Effective Schools for Disaffected Students: Integration and Segregation,* Routledge: London.

Cooper, P, Smith, C J and Upton, G (1994) *Emotional and Behavioural Difficulties: From Theory to Practice,* Routledge: London.

Cooper, P and McIntyre, D (1993) 'Commonality in teachers' and pupils' perceptions of effective learning,' *British Journal of Educational Psychology,* Vol. 63 (pp. 381-399).

Cooper, P and McIntyre, D (1994a) 'Teachers' and pupils' perceptions of effective classroom learning,' in M Hughes (ed) *Perceptions of Teaching and Learning,* Multilingual Matters: Clevedon.

Cooper, P and McIntyre, D (1994b) 'Patterns of interaction between teachers' and students' classroom thinking, and their implications for the provision of learning opportunities,' *Teaching and Teacher Education,* Vol. 10, No. 6 (pp. 633-646).

Cooper, P and McIntyre, D (1994c) 'The importance of power sharing in classroom learning,' in M Hughes (ed) *Teaching and Learning in Changing Times,* Blackwell: Oxford.

Abbreviations

ADD	Attention Deficit Disorder
ADHD	Attention Deficit Hyperactivity Disorder
AT	Attainment Target
BST	Behaviour Support Teacher
CSE	Certificate of Secondary Education
DfE	Department for Education
EBD	Emotional and behavioural difficulties
ESW	Educational Social Worker
EWO	Educational Welfare Officer
FE	further education
GCSE	General Certificate of Secondary Education
HMI	Her Majesty's Inspectorate
INSET	inservice training
IT	information technology
LEA	Local Education Authority
LSA	Learning Support Assistant
LSC	Learning Support Co-ordinator
MLD	moderate learning difficulty
MSA	midday supervisory assistant
NCT	National Curriculum Test
PE	physical education
PRU	Pupil Referral Unit
RE	religious education
SAT	Standard Assessment Task
SEN	special educational needs
SNAST	Special Needs Advisory and Support Teacher
TVEI	Technical and Vocational Education Initiative

Index